With Captain Stairs to Katanga

Slavery and subjugation in the Congo 1891-92

WILLIAM STAIRS

WITH CAPTAIN STAIRS

TO KATANGA

BY

JOSEPH A. MOLONEY, L.R.C.P., F.R.G.S.

MEDICAL OFFICER OF THE EXPEDITION.

WITH ILLUSTRATIONS AND MAP

LONDON:
SAMPSON LOW, MARSTON & COMPANY
LIMITED,
St. Dunstan's House,
FETTER LANE, FLEET STREET, E.C.
1893.

[*All rights reserved.*]

Cover design copyright © Chris Eason 2007. Front cover image *Congo Pirogue*, ©2006 focalplane.com, reproduced by kind permission of Paul Ashton.

First published 1893 as *With Captain Stairs to Katanga*, Joseph A. Moloney; Sampson Low, Marston & Co., London.

This edition published by Jeppestown Press, 10A Scawfell St, London, E2 8NG, United Kingdom.

Editing, arrangement, notes and introduction copyright © David Saffery 2007

ISBN   0-9553936-5-5
ISBN-13 978-0-9553936-5-5

All Rights Reserved. No part of this publication may be reproduced, stored in a retrieval system, or transmitted, in any form or by any means, electronic, mechanical, photocopying, recording, scanning or otherwise, except as described below, without the permission in writing of the Publisher. Copying is not permitted except for personal use, to the extent permitted by national copyright law. Requests for permission for other kinds of copying, such as copying for general distribution, for advertising or promotional purposes, for creating new collective works, or for resale, and other enquiries, should be addressed to the Publisher.

With Captain Stairs to Katanga

Slavery and subjugation in the Congo 1891-92

By Joseph A. Moloney
Introduction and notes by David Saffery

JOSEPH A. MOLONEY

Contents

Contents	vii
Introduction to 2007 edition	ix
Route of the Stairs Expedition	xiii
Preface	xv
The Katanga Company	17
Zanzibar and Bagamoyo	27
Usagara and Mpwapwa	35
Ugogo and Unyamyembe	45
Tabora	57
Ugunda and Ugalla	67
Karema	83
Murungu	93
Across the Lualaba	107
Msiri	123
The Fight	131
Fort Bunkeya	139
To Tanganyika	159
To the Coast	173
Bibliography	188

Introduction to 2007 Edition

The Stairs expedition was a Victorian imperial adventure led by a Canadian-born soldier, engineer and mercenary, William Grant Stairs, whose first experience of Central Africa was as second-in-command of Henry Morton Stanley's 1887 expedition to the southern Sudan to relieve Emin Pasha, made when Stairs was aged just 25. Over the following three years Stairs trekked extensively in Africa; nearly died from a wound inflicted by a poisoned arrow; and became one of the first white people to ascend the Rwenzori mountains on the Ugandan-Congolese border.

In 1891, Stairs was commissioned by the Katanga Company to lead a military expedition to Bunkeya in Katanga, in the south of the Congo region, to obtain the subjugation of Msiri, a Nyamwezi trader-turned-ruler who, armed initially only with a few guns, had seized power in about 1860 and subsequently ruled over the trade and inhabitants of much of the Luapula valley (although Moloney suggests that by 1891 Msiri's empire had contracted to only around 14 square miles). The mineral riches of Katanga were irresistibly attractive to Europeans; from the north, King Leopold II of Belgium was determined to add Katanga to the territory of his own personal fiefdom, the Congo Free State; while in the south of the continent Cecil Rhodes told one of the agents of the British South Africa Company, "I want you to get M'siri's. I mean Katanga. ... You must go and get Katanga."[1]

Msiri resisted the blandishments of the British South Africa Company, in the form of a treaty delivered to him for signature by Alfred Sharpe, British Vice-Consul in Nyasaland. Shortly after Sharpe's departure from Bunkeya, a modest Belgian military force arrived at Bunkeya under the command of Paul le Marinel, and was permitted to establish a small post near Msiri's capital, although Msiri refused to accept any formal treaty with the

---

[1] Rhodes to Joseph Thomson, quoted in Rotberg, R., *Journal of African History*, Vol. 5, No. 2. (1964), p290

Belgians. Six months later, in October 1891, Alexandre Delcommune arrived in Bunkeya with a second Belgian expedition. Again he tried to secure the submission of Msiri to Belgian rule: and again Msiri refused.

In December, Stairs arrived from Zanzibar at the head of a column of 336 black porters and armed askaris. His second-in-command was a young Belgian soldier from Antwerp, Omer Bodson; third-in-command was a French aristocrat, the Marquis de Bonchamps; a former Grenadier Guardsman, Thomas Robinson, attended the party as general factotum; and the author of this book, Joseph Augustus Moloney, served as expedition medical officer. Once in Bunkeya, Stairs demanded that Msiri fly the flag of the Congo Free State as a token of his acceptance of Leopold II's sovereignty over Katanga. Msiri refused, and fled Bunkeya for the nearby village of Munema, the home of his favourite wife; Stairs resolved to arrest him, and sent Bodson and de Bonchamps to Munema with a force of 115 askaris.

What happened next is less than wholly clear: an 1893 article in the French magazine *Le Tour du Monde*, based on de Bonchamps' notes, reported that Bodson proceeded into the village with a small group of men to negotiate, was attacked by Msiri and shot him dead in self-defence, before being himself fatally wounded by one of Msiri's servants. Moloney—who was not present at the action in Munema—reports the same story.

Moloney also states that Msiri's body was brought back to Stairs before being returned to his sons for burial. Dan Crawford, a missionary at the mission station of the Plymouth Brethren at Bunkeya, reported in his autobiography published twenty years later that the askaris "were so maddened by what had taken place that they cut Mushidi's [Msiri's] head from its trunk and carried it on a pole back to the camp"[2], before transporting it in a petrol tin back to the East African coast. This is partly confirmed by de Bonchamps, who reported that "We also carried the corpse of Msiri, whose head was immediately hoisted at the top of a raised stake, in full view of the inhabitants of the country." («Nous

---

[2] Crawford, D., *Thinking Black*, p307-8

emportâmes aussi le cadavre de Msiri, dont la tête fut immédiatement hissée au sommet d'un pieu élevé, bien en vue des habitants du pays »). Of the march back from Munema to Bunkeya, Moloney says only that "I happened to glance at the dead man's face. It seemed to wear a mocking smile which, somehow, was not easily forgotten."

In the aftermath of Msiri's assassination, his empire collapsed, and the area came under Belgian rule as part of the province of Katanga.

So, what makes Moloney's testimony interesting? Why is his experience in Africa relevant to a twenty-first century reader?

The answer lies partly in Moloney's position—his place at the centre of the action, which gives modern readers a unique, first-person view of the sordid, shabby race between European states that characterised the colonial division of Africa; part of a world where the lives of black Africans were, to all intents and purposes, worthless, and where the East African slave trade still pervaded everyday life.

This conflict between external political powers fought out in Africa is, in its essence, paralleled by the Cold War, during which the same territory, known first as the Democratic Republic of the Congo and then as Zaire, became a client of the West; and its ruler, Mobutu Sese Seko, formed the embodiment of a new form of authoritarian rule based on personal greed, brutality and the shameless abuse of the country's resources, christened 'kleptocracy'. It is not unreasonable to trace a direct line of descent from Stairs and his party, who effectively helped to annex Katanga in 1891, to the white mercenaries hired 70 years later to support the government of Moise Tshombe, president of Katanga during its short-lived secession; while, in terms of cynicism coupled with rapacity, there is little to choose between the Katanga Company, which hired Stairs, and the Western governments and multinational companies which propped up the Mobutu regime for over 30 years.

Joseph Augustus Moloney was born in Newry, Northern Ireland in 1857, the son of a junior army officer, an Irishman who settled in Kingston in Surrey; his surname suggests that he was probably an Irish Roman Catholic. Moloney studied medicine at the King and Queen's College of Physicians, Dublin, and at St Thomas's Hospital in Waterloo, and practised in South London, where family accounts suggest that he was held in high esteem, especially by his less wealthy patients. The same family accounts describe Moloney as "hard as nails" and a keen sportsman. He is believed to have served in the 1881 Anglo-Boer War in South Africa; after the Stairs expedition he joined the Katanga Company's rival, the British South Africa Company, and commanded an expedition to the Company's territories in the Luangwa Valley in Zambia in 1895. He died the following year at home in Surbiton, aged only 38; his obituary in the Geographical Journal suggesting that his early death could be ascribed to the hardships he had suffered in Africa.

Like other Victorian writers from the imperial *milieu*, Moloney is an uneasy guide for a modern reader. Hostile towards black people, Jews and Germans, and demonstrating a patronising tolerance of the French, Moloney's habitual use of the word 'nigger' was berated at the time of this book's original publication by no less a critic than Henry Morton Stanley, who described it as "ugly and derisive".

While, in partial mitigation, one may plead that this book reflects the prevailing racist, ethnocentric attitude of many white travellers to Africa at the time, Moloney's bigotry and anti-Semitism pervade the narrative; perhaps unconsciously reflecting the desperate personal insecurity of a young, middle-class Irish Catholic attempting to build a career in a Victorian society where Catholics were still viewed with suspicion and mistrust.[*] On reflection, I have chosen to keep his original text in its entirety, changing only some common place-names for their modern equivalents; while I recognise that this may not please all readers, I believe that an unbowdlerised narrative makes it easier to view in its proper context the particular version of African history that this book portrays.

D.S. 2007

---

[*] Roman Catholics were not permitted to become Members of Parliament or crown servants until the Catholic Emancipation Act was passed in 1829, just 28 years before Moloney was born.

Route of the Stairs Expedition

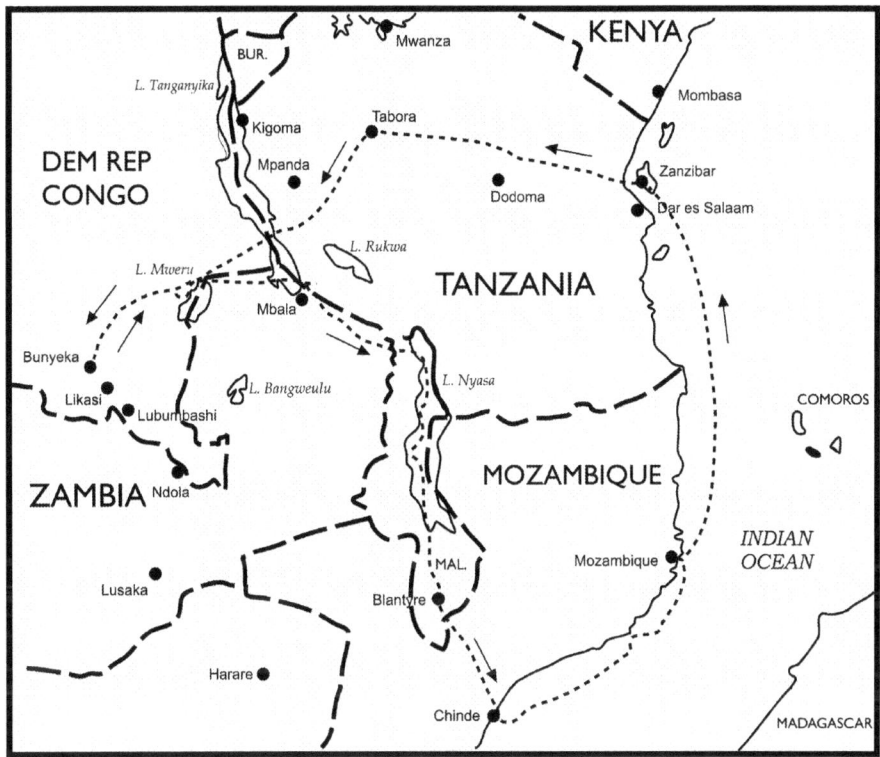

The Stairs Expedition left Zanzibar on 27 June 1891 and trekked west for 900 miles, reaching Bunyeka on 14 December 1891. From Lake Mweru, the expedition travelled south-east for over a thousand miles towards the Portuguese port of Chinde, where Stairs died on 9 June 1892. The survivors reached Zanzibar on 20 June 1892.

Preface

THE following pages have been written from a diary which I kept while serving on the Stairs expedition, and their object is to give a faithful record of that adventure. I have much pleasure in expressing my obligations to my friend, Mr. Lloyd Sanders, who has afforded me much valuable help in the production of the volume. While the book has been passing through the press, many things have happened in the German and Belgian spheres through which we travelled. In the first place Herr von Siegl's successor at Tabora has defeated and killed Seke, an event that should certainly tend to the strengthening of Teutonic authority. Captain Jacques will soon, I trust, be delivered from his perilous position by the arrival of reinforcements; but I see no reason to qualify my statements as to the inadequacy of his original resources, or on the criminality of the Portuguese and German connivance in the smuggling of arms and ammunition by the Arabs.

Again the Delcommune and Bia expeditions are on their way home, leaving M. Legat as the representative of the Congo State in Katanga. The former, in the course of its wanderings, has made a welcome addition to our geographical knowledge by exploring the Lukungu and identifying the true source of the Congo. In spite of the lamented death of its commandant, the Bia caravan appears to have done some excellent work in surveying the western shores of Lakes Mweru and Bangweulu. Lieutenant Franqui's report will therefore be awaited with general interest, and the survivors of the Stairs expedition feel a special desire to know how that country prospers which their gallant leader delivered from the ruthless despotism of Msiri.

I take this opportunity of offering my thanks to the Englishmen who befriended us in Zanzibar and elsewhere. Besides those whose names occur in the following pages, I must express my particular gratitude to Mr. Nicol, of the firm of Messrs. Smith, Mackenzie and Co.

Chapter I

The Katanga Company

The Katanga project—First meeting with Captain Stairs—The Katanga Company—Its relations with the Congo Free State—Reports of gold in Katanga—The country's healthiness and fertility—M. le Marinel's expedition—Lieutenant Legat—The Delcommune expedition—Objects of the Stairs expedition—Mr. Sharpe and Mr. Joseph Thomson—The question of valid occupation—Choice of route—The Bia expedition—My companions: Captain Stairs, Captain Bodson, the Marquis de Bonchamps, and Mr. Robinson—Mixed staffs and international syndicates.

IN May, 1890, I returned to England from a tour in Morocco, undertaken chiefly for purposes of sport. Greatly to my delight, I heard a few months afterwards, that Captain Stairs, who had acquired fame as one of Mr. H. M. Stanley's lieutenants, was organizing an expedition to Katangaland, and that he had not as yet, secured a medical officer. My application for the appointment was immediately despatched, and there came a reply, by return of post, asking me to call upon the Captain at his hotel.

I must confess that the tall, fair, and delicate-looking young man, whom I found seated in the coffee-room, appeared, at first sight, very unlike the typical African traveller; but his interrogatory showed, at any rate, that he did not waste time in beating about the bush. "Can you shoot?" he asked; and when the question had been answered in the affirmative, there came a second and apparently subsidiary query, "Have you brought your testimonials?" After a rapid glance at those documents, Captain Stairs informed me that my capacities for the undertaking seemed superior to those of his other correspondents—of whom the number was by no means small—and that, if no objection was raised from Brussels, he would be happy to accept my services. Then he wrote out a list of my kit, and we parted after a talk that had taken up a bare twenty minutes. In due course the nomination was confirmed, and thus I found myself enrolled as medical officer to the Katangaland expedition.

The Katanga Company, whose employment I had entered, is an international syndicate, which was originally founded as an offshoot of the Commercial and Industrial Company of the Congo. British opulence was represented on the directorate, in the first instance, by Sir William Mackinnon, and Sir John Kirke; French, by the Parisian banker, M. Bunau-Varilla; and Belgian, by M Lambert de Rothschild, the Brussels Bank, and so forth. It were unnecessary to weary the reader with the financial aspects of the project or the negotiations for its formation. Enough, that the capital of the company amounted to three million francs, that Commander Cameron, the celebrated African traveller, effected the amalgamation of the British and Continental interests, and that the convention, with the Congo Free State, was signed the 12th of March, 1891.

Now that document, as published in the *Mouvement Geographique*, runs to portentous lengths; accordingly, the following brief summary of its terms seems sufficient for purposes of explanation. The Free State made over to the Katanga Company, for twenty years, certain preferential rights over the mines reputed to be situated in the countries of Katanga and Urua; or, in other words, in that portion of the State's dominions which forms the basin of the Upper Congo above Riba-Riba. It also conceded, in full ownership, a third of the territory belonging to the public domain within those limits. In return the company undertook to establish within three years' time two steamers, either on the confluents of the Upper Congo, or on the lakes adjacent to the Free State. Secondly, it promised to construct, within the same period, at least three stations within the conceded area. Thirdly, a pledge was given that the association would organize a police-force strong enough to protect its boats and forts; and this constabulary was to be liable, on demand, to service under the Free State. Lastly, the Katanga Company undertook to give every assistance towards the suppression of the slave trade, and to prevent the importation of spirits and weapons of war. These terms, it will be observed, do not differ greatly from the privileges conceded to our own chartered societies.

It would be futile to deny that the precious metals, and particularly gold, formed the main objects of the Company's solicitude. I leave others to descant upon the considerations of abstract morality involved in the quest, and will confine myself to the inquiry how far the existence of the *irritatementa malorum* could be considered proven. To most minds the evidence will appear very fairly conclusive, though actual experiment was naturally wanting as to their discovery in workable quantities. Thus, in his well-known book, *Across Africa*, Commander Cameron describes how Haméd ibn Hamed, an Arab trader, whom he met at Nyangwé, had produced a calabash holding about a quartful of nuggets, varying in size from the top of the little finger to a swanshot.

"I asked him," wrote the explorer, "whence they came, and he said that some of his slaves at Katanga found them while clearing out a water-hole, and brought them to him, thinking that they might do for shot. He said he had not looked for more, as he did not know such little bits were of any use. The natives, too, knew of the gold, but it is so soft that they do not value it, preferring 'the red copper to the white.' I heard, when at Benguela, that gold had been found in copper brought from Katanga, and that a company was buying all the Katanga copper it could obtain in order to extract the gold. From a man in Urua I bought a silver bracelet produced in or near this district. Cinnabar is found in large quantities in Urua, near the capital of Kasongo. Copper is also found in large quantities at Katanga, and for a considerable distance to the westward."

The gallant voyager's assertions with regard to gold had been confirmed since the establishment of the Congo Free State by the numerous presents of that metal made by Arab merchants to the Belgian officials. Besides Major Cambier, who was stationed on Lake Tanganyika from 1877 to 1880, had frequently heard both Arabs and natives declare that much gold was found in Katanga.

The fertility of the soil, and the salubrity of the climate, had been described in enthusiastic periods by the Portuguese Senhor Ivens, and his French Companion M. Capello, by the German Herr Reichard, and by the English missionary Mr. Arnot. The last witness gives a most spirited account in his book, *Gazenganze*, of his two years' residence in the country (1886, 1887). According to him the temperature is capable of extreme heat without becoming oppressive; the atmosphere is always clear, and not befouled by fogs as in the Barotsé country. M. Capello, in a lecture delivered before the Paris Geographical Society, waxed eloquent upon the abundant water-supply of the Lualaba and the Luapula, and the wonderful heaviness of the crops. Clearly the Company was justified, even with allowance made for optimism and exaggeration, in believing that Katangaland would recoup a substantial outlay. It is true that such calculations fail to take the indigenous nigger into account, and the nigger, as these pages will show, can never be wholly omitted from the reckoning whether of profit or, more generally, of loss.

Several attempts had already been made to give validity to the paper-ownership of the Katanga district, as allotted to the Free State under the General Act of the Berlin Conference. On the 23rd of December, 1890, Lieutenant Paul le Marinel was despatched from Lusambo, a fort constructed by him on the Upper Sankuru (a tributary of the Kasai, which river flows into the Congo) to hoist the Belgian flag over Bunkeya, the capital of the country. Under him was a force some three hundred strong, with MM. Descamps, Legat, and Verdiekt, as its lieutenants. The expedition marched along the Lubi, through a region hitherto unknown to Europeans. It appeared densely populated, and its inhabitants are described in M. le Manuel's report as affecting the most extraordinary method of dressing their hair, besides bedaubing their faces with various pigments. The Balungu tribe, dwelling upon the Kanioka, has reached an elementary civilization, and is addicted to commerce and the cultivation of the soil. Evading an effort on the part of the chief Muzembe to bar the way, the adventurers crossed the Sankuru and reached the source of the Lothimni, travelling over a plateau which, according to le Marinel, is well-watered and abounds in game. In March the passage of the Lualaba was affected by means of native canoes, and on the right bank they were met by a representative of Msiri the king of Katangaland. Pressing southward Lieutenant le Marinel traversed a mountainous tract, where dwell curious tribes of troglodytes, and crossing the plains arrived on the 18th of April, 1891, at Bunkeya. He was most courteously received by the aged potentate, and strengthened his cause by various gifts of clothing and ornaments. With great difficulty he extracted from the wily negro a letter, couched in the most ambiguous terms, which appeared to acknowledge King Leopold's overlordship. Msiri, however, declined to make a definite act of submission or to hoist the Belgian flag. Finally, after a seven weeks' stay at Bunkeya, M. le Marinel retraced his steps to Lusambo where he arrived safe and sound on the 11th of August. Lieutenant Legat with a garrison of Dahomeyan soldiers, was left behind in a fort built upon the Lifoi, some three marches from the capital, to watch the development of events.

Secondly, the Commercial and Industrial Company of the Congo had equipped an expedition under M. Alexandre Delcommune which, on the formation of the Katanga syndicate, passed into its service. The objects of the enterprise were partly to effect a settlement of the country, but chiefly to discover gold. M. Delcommune's instructions were that he should repair to Bunkeya, and, if possible, persuade Msiri to accept the flag; and then advance, without loss of time, to the south, where the gold-fields were reported to lie. His acquaintance with Africa dated from 1873, and he was accompanied by a competent staff, of whom Lieutenant Hakanson, a Swede, served as second in command, M. Diderich as engineer and M. Briart as doctor. But the route selected, that of the Lualaba, with Bena-Kamba as its starting-point, proved extremely unfortunate. The caravan, which left that post on the 30th of January, 1891, encountered rapid after rapid. Six canoes were lost, and subsequently the steel boat foundered and had to be abandoned. The commander of the caravan had some hairbreadth escapes, now from an infuriated hippo, and again from sunken rocks and treacherous currents. Still, certain stretches of the river proved navigable, and M. Delcommune, as he advanced, made the acquaintance of some interesting tribes, particularly the Wacheni, a warlike race that has never submitted to the Arab yoke. On the 3rd of May the expedition arrived at N'Gongo-Lutita, where it was fortunate enough to encounter Rachid, Tippoo-Tib's nephew and successor. This friendly Arab provided some welcome supplies of porters, bringing Delcommune's strength up to 350 all told. After a fortnight's rest, he started for Katanga overland. No detailed report of his proceedings has since been published, but his progress appears to have been fairly uneventful, and numerous treaties were concluded with the chiefs on the road. Travelling by way of Niambo, Lake Kassali and probably Lake Upamba, he attained Bunkeya in October. We subsequently gathered from M. Legat that Msiri had received the strangers with his customary courtesy, but equally, according to his wont, had declined to accept the Belgian flag. M. Delcommune accordingly pushed southwards in search of the auriferous drifts. I shall deal later on with our efforts to open communications with him, and with his subsequent adventures.

The Stairs expedition may be considered in some respects supplementary to that of Delcommune. Our objects, however, were essentially political; that to say, we proposed to secure the country, either with or without Msiri's leave, for the Congo Free State. Nor could we allow time to run to waste, otherwise the claim stood in considerable danger of being "jumped". For other eyes besides Belgian had been turned towards this desirable and derelict territory, those, namely, of Mr. Cecil Rhodes, the guiding spirit of the British South Africa Company Already one of its agents, Mr. Alfred Sharpe, now H.M. vice-consul in Nyasaland, had reached Msiri's capital and had attempted to elicit information as to the gold deposits, also, if rumour does not err, to exact a treaty. Certain it is that he spent a week in negotiating with the crafty king; and Captain Stairs was subsequently informed by the English missionaries at Bunkeya that, on his departure in November, 1890, *re infecta**, Mr. Sharpe had left with Mr. Swan, one of their number, an act of submission to be signed by Msiri, in case the royal mind should change. Further there were stories abroad that a second effort to attain the same goal would shortly be made by Mr. Joseph Thomson the well-known explorer of Masailand and the Upper Niger. As a matter of fact, the latter's mission, if really undertaken, never emerged from the state of conception and preparation. I have been informed, however, that he was compelled to suspend his preparations by the orders of the Foreign Office, and in any case there was presumption that Mr. Rhodes's ambition would not recoil from a repetition against the Belgians of the tactics that had served him so admirably with the Portuguese, in Manicaland. Accordingly the Stairs expedition resolved itself, as we imagined, into a race for Bunkeya against such formidable competitors as the officers of the British South Africa Company.

Upon this delicate topic I may remark that, in my humble judgment, Mr. Cecil Rhodes, even if his reputed purpose had been carried to completeness, would have been acting within the letter of the law. For the General Act of the Brussels Conference distinctly stipulates that all occupation by European powers in Africa must be valid; that is to say, it must possess the outward signs of treaties, the national flag, and a sufficient police to ensure the preservation of order. Now, it would be futile to deny that though the Free State had been possessed for several years of the paper ownership of the Upper

---

* With the matter still to be completed. DS

Congo basin, yet a poverty of resources had prevented more than the feeblest efforts to make good the title. I remember that, shortly before we started, several English newspapers, notably the Morning Post, urged with considerable cogency that, in consequence of this proved incapacity, Msiri's kingdom should be regarded as a no-man's-land, liable to seizure by the first corner. And no doubt the argument is cogent enough so far as it goes. At the same time, the civilized States would obviously be pursuing a short-sighted policy did they forget the duty of standing firmly together against the Negro, and, more particularly, the Arab. If outlying strips are to be freely snapped up, where is the process to end? May it not happen that while the British South Africa Company gains by the scramble, the East Africa and Niger find their boundaries rigidly circumscribed? Think again of the international complications that would attend a collision between British and, say, Germans, or—as in our somewhat abnormal instance—between Englishmen serving under their own flag and Englishmen enlisted by a foreign sovereign. Surely patience should be exercised by all concerned, until Africa passes from its present artificial partition to the Powers that can both colonize and administer. At the risk of wrecking my argument, I may say that Belgium is hardly likely to be reckoned in that category.

Speed being an essential to our undertaking, the choice of route was of necessity a matter for anxious consideration. The easiest and best approach lay via the Zambesi and Shire, Lake Nyasa and the Stevenson road, to the south end of Tanganyika. Mr. H. H. Johnston, however, the Imperial Commissioner for Nyasaland, reported that, owing to Arab disturbances, the way could not be considered practicable for the time being; and that no transport was available. Accordingly, the directors decided that we should proceed across German territory to Karema, cross Lake Tanganyika, and then descend upon Bunkeya from the north-east. The company also determined on sending yet another caravan to reinforce Captain Stairs in case of hostilities, and to take over the permanent administration of the country. Captain Bia, formerly of the Belgian army, was placed in command, with Lieutenant Franqui as his second. They embarked at Antwerp on the 18th of May, with instructions to make for Katanga by le Marinel's route, namely, that of the Upper Sankuru. We shall meet them again in the neighbourhood of Bunkeya.

A word in conclusion of these preliminary remarks as to my commander and companions. Captain William Grant Stairs had, as the most cursory observer of current events must be aware, already won for himself an illustrious name in the annals of African exploration. He was born on the 1st of July, 1863, in Halifax, Nova Scotia, and educated partly at Murchiston College, Edinburgh, and partly at the Military College of Kingston, Canada. Having passed with distinction through the engineering department, he accepted employment on a New Zealand railway. Coming to England, he availed himself of a regulation whereby commissions in the Royal Engineers were thrown open to certain colonial academies, and was gazetted in 1885. He was serving with his regiment when, in the autumn of 1886, Mr. Stanley's expedition was organized for the relief of Emin Pasha. Lieutenant Stairs sent in the first application for an engagement on the staff; his offer was promptly accepted, and he obtained leave of absence from Lord Wolseley. Upon his exploits during that memorable enterprise I feel exempt from dilating, since they are a matter of common knowledge. Every one will remember his tactfulness and resource at Fort Bodo, his rescue of Parke and Nelson from starvation, his ascent of Mount Rwenzori and discovery of the true sources of the Nile. His was, wrote Mr. Stanley, "one of those rare personalities, oftener visible among military men than among civilians, who could obey orders without argument, who could accept a command, and without ado or fuss execute it religiously; courageous, careful, watchful, diligent and faithful." Shortly after his return, Lieutenant Stairs exchanged from the Engineers into the Royal Welsh Regiment, with the rank of captain. But he soon grew weary of life at Aldershot, and gladly accepted the Katanga Company's offer to lead one of its expeditions. He was fully conscious of the rashness of the experiment, since his constitution had been severely tried by malaria and exertion, nor was its tone entirely restored. Indeed, before leaving England, he told more than one of his friends that they might never see him again. Wedded to action, and burning to excel, Captain Stairs felt that the trophies of Mr. Stanley would not suffer him to sleep.

As second in command went Captain Bodson, an officer of the Belgian Carbineers. He was born at Antwerp on the 5th of January, 1856, and after a spell of military service, accepted an appointment under the Congo Free State, in 1887. Upon that river he displayed remarkable dash and competency to meet emergencies. At first attached to the topographical brigade at Mateba, he was stationed for three years at the Stanley Falls. There he gave considerable assistance to the Emin Relief Expedition during its march up-country, and presided over the court-martial which tried the murderer of the unfortunate Major Barttelot. Captain Bodson was next transferred to Léopoldville, and then to Basoko. Recalled to Belgium about 1889, he distinguished himself in the suppression of the Liege riots, and received the personal thanks of the king.

Of the other Europeans, the Marquis de Bonchamps was some thirty-two years of age, and had served in a French cavalry regiment. He had been a great traveller and sportsman, notably among the Rocky Mountains, where he spent several seasons in pursuit of big game. Concerning myself, I may say that I had practised for several years as a doctor in the south of London, and, as has been mentioned already, an expedition to Morocco had given me some slight experience of African travel. Lastly, we took with us Mr. Robinson, formerly a private in the Grenadier Guards, as carpenter and general factotum. His testimonials gave promise of pluck and steadiness, nor, as the sequel will show, did they at all belie his character.

The reader will observe that we were a mixed staff acting under an international syndicate. On the whole I am inclined to pronounce that such enterprises are less likely to succeed than those conducted on more homogeneous lines. Political considerations naturally cause a company thus constituted to adopt a somewhat flabby and vacillating policy. Still more certain is it that differences of race are accentuated by the worries and fatigue of a long march overland, and that the small band splits into yet smaller cliques— Britons on the one side and Continentals on the other. The world, however, has grown rather tired of the quarrels and jealousies that are the inevitable concomitants of hazardous endeavours. Accordingly, I do not propose to recur again to this unpleasant topic; still, the existence of some unnecessary friction on the Stairs expedition cannot be wholly ignored.

Chapter II

Zanzibar and Bagamoyo

We start in the *Madura*—Mombasa—Zanzibar—Bodson at Dar-es-Salaam—Departure of the Juba—An audience with the sultan—Hiring a boy—Abdullah—Engagement of porters— Free or slave labour—Composition of the caravan—Off to Bagamoyo—German administration—Our men at large—An undisputed eviction—Arrival of Bodson and Stairs—The German officers and the French mission—Emin Pasha's daughter, Captain Jacques, and Mr. Stokes.

ON the 11th of May, Captain Bodson, Robinson, and I bade farewell to our friends at the Albert Docks, and embarked on board the *Madura*, of the British India Steamship Company. We took with us Mr. Stanley's black boy, Saleh, who had determined to return to his native Zanzibar, and the young gentleman's airs and graces afforded much entertainment. Captain Stairs proceeded overland with the Marquis de Bonchamps, and met the ship at Naples.

I do not propose to encumber these pages with the hackneyed incidents of a passage down the Mediterranean and through the canal. Enough, that on the 11th of June we put into the fine harbour of the island of Mombasa, and subsequently visited the Church Missionary Society's plantations at Freetown, where the somewhat dubious experiment of inducing the nigger to work without the stick is being tried with a fair measure of success. Our stay, however, was chiefly occupied in hiring porters for the caravan, and, with some difficulty, 116 capable men were induced to throw in their lot with the expedition. These we shipped across to Zanzibar on the 14th, and, late in the afternoon, the *Madura* steamed into the bustling port, through crowds of dhows and shipping of all sorts and sizes. We landed and repaired to the Criterion Hotel, as to which establishment my diary records some impressions the reverse of complimentary. A stroll round the town resulted in the conclusion that, though Zanzibar undoubtedly shows signs of progress, its present buildings are little superior to those of an ordinary eastern city, the Sultan's palace being peculiarly insignificant. We noticed numerous Hindus and Banyans, who have been attracted to the island by the development of trade, and who furnish a most welcome supply of skilled labour.

A visit to the *Madura*, next morning, was attended by a somewhat unpleasant discovery. The porters hired at Mombasa had fallen out among themselves during the night, fighting like wild cats, and using their knives freely. Fortunately no great damage was done, still, as they were evidently an unruly set, and extremely likely to desert with the three months' wages paid in advance, if exposed to the temptations of their friends and relatives, Captain Stairs determined to get them out of harm's way. Accordingly a dhow was chartered, and Captain Bodson undertook to convey the whole contingent to the German port of Dar-es-Salaam on the mainland, and rejoin us before the start from Bagamoyo. I helped him to get them on board, and a difficult job it was. Captain Bodson called over the names as the men passed over the side, while I stood on deck to see that they did not escape. The stowage of so many unwilling forms into a thirty-eight feet boat proved no easy business, and the ingenuous manner in which some of the fellows shouted, "Coming, master, coming," while moving at a snail's pace towards the bows, might have amused a disinterested spectator, but taxed the patience of those superintending the operation. However the dhow was under way by four p.m., and Bodson bade us a cheery adieu. We afterwards heard that he experienced a most tiresome passage, as the vessel took two days and a half in making the distance of forty-eight miles.

Our tactics with regard to the porters were distinctly justified on the 20th, when the S.S. *Juba*, of the Imperial East Africa Company started for Mozambique with a caravan of one hundred and fifty bearers commanded by Lieutenant Sclater, RE., and accompanied by Mr. Whyte, naturalist, When the ship prepared to weigh anchor, she was surrounded by a perfect flotilla of shore boats, hovering round to pick up any double-dealing porter who thought fit to jump overboard with his three months' pay. Fortunately a steam launch of H.M.S. *Conquest* came to the rescue, and the officer, after due warning given, charged the interlopers and sank some five of them. No loss of life ensued, as the niggers can swim like fishes. Then the blue-jackets, armed with single-sticks, dealt some shrewd blows to the right and left on the thick Zanzibari pates. After this gentle admonition the would-be rescue party sheered off, and the *Juba* steamed out of harbour followed by the cheers of the people on shore. The expedition, which served the African Lakes Company, was bound for the interior of British Central Africa, via the Zambesi and Shire, with the prospect of an overland journey of a hundred miles or so.

On the previous day, Lieutenant Sclater and the European members of our expedition had been admitted to an audience with the Sultan. We assembled outside the British consulate at half-past ten a.m., Captain Stairs in the uniform of the Welsh regiment, Lieutenant Sclater in that of the Engineers, the Marquis and myself in evening dress. There we were met by the acting Consul-General, in the absence of Sir Gerald Portal, and conducted in procession through the streets, preceded by a bodyguard of Zanzibaris attired in red and sleeveless shell-jackets and flowing lower skirts. The natives, knowing it to be *levée* day, lined the streets and saluted us with a fire of pungent criticism. Inside the palace yard were drawn up seven hundred of the Sultan's troops—the total strength of his army being eleven hundred men—while his band, recruited from the Portuguese settlement of Goa in India, played "God save the Queen". His Highness, a swarthy and intellectual-looking man of about forty, met us at the top of the grand staircase, and we followed him through a doorway and down a long chamber. Next he seated himself, with Captain Stairs and the rest of us on his right. Sherbert appeared, to be sipped as a matter of etiquette, followed by coffee. Then the Sultan addressed some brief remarks to each of us, invoked the blessing of Allah upon our enterprise, and promised us every assistance in his power. He accompanied us to the landing, and there took his leave. As we emerged from the palace the band struck up the Zanzibari national anthem, with its peculiarly Eastern cadence of melancholy defiance. The whole ceremony was intensely Oriental, and even the unaccustomed sensation of being in dress clothes at midday failed to invest our proceedings with any particular sense of the ridiculous.

Our evenings passed pleasantly enough, as the residents and officers of the various British vessels vied with one another in kindness and hospitality. Indeed, so pressing were the attentions of our late messmates, that the Marquis de Bonchamps and I were in some danger of being taken home again in the *Madura*. Owing to the non-arrival of our boat, we did not get off the ship until she was passing H.M.S. *Conquest*, much to the anxiety of Captain Stairs, though we were prepared, in the last emergency, to swim ashore. During the daytime I had little to do except to complete my outfit and hire a boy. The latter necessity proved difficult of attainment, as the specimens which presented themselves were anything but satisfactory. I asked one of them if he was married, "Yes," was the answer. "Have you any children?" "No; but God has three which He will send at the proper time."

Despite this pious waiting upon Providence, I sent the gentleman away, and finally lighted upon a treasure in Abdullah, on the recommendation of Mr. Robertson, head of the custom-house. He was a Manyuema by birth, extremely intelligent, a great ladies' man, but lax on the score of honesty.

Captain Stairs, with the assistance of our agents, Messrs. Smith, Mackenzie and Co., was busily engaged during the week in engaging porters to make up the full complement of our caravan. As there has been much discussion of late upon the employment of slave labour on expeditions like ours, I may say that we tried honestly to secure free men. Indeed Captain Stairs took every *pagazi* (porter) before the Sultan and British Consul to make a declaration of freedom. At the same time the Arabs were conspicuously present at the hiring of the men, acting as intermediaries, and calling attention to their merits. "Here is a fine fat fellow," one would say; and another, "This boy can walk many miles without fatigue." How far these persons could be styled masters, and how far middlemen merely, it would be difficult to say. My own impression is that you cannot abolish an immemorial custom like slavery by a stroke of the pen. The Arab has for generations exercised an ascendancy over the Zanzibari, which the latter has come to regard as part of the essential scheme of things. With the nigger's imitative instinct, he models manners and deportment on his owner's, who, besides, treats him in return with much tact and consideration. A generation hence, the coast natives may have come to take themselves very seriously indeed. In the meantime, I suspect that they will make little use of their newly fledged liberties, and that domestic servitude will flourish, though in an unauthorized shape, with all the luxuriance of former years.

Our safari (caravan) comprised 336 men all told, of whom 116 were recruited Mombasa and 220 at Zanzibar. They were a mixed multitude, of whom the majority proclaimed itself Zanzibari by its corpulence of form and voluble use of the Swahili or littoral language. Others were Wasakuma hailing from the south end of Lake Victoria, and the remainder, for most part, Wanyamwesi from Unyanyembe, still nearer the equator. Both these contingents had contracted Zanzibari habits, and had exchanged the primitive loin-cloth for long flowing robes; but of the two the Wanyamwesi proved decidedly the superior. They were finely built men, and, unlike the Zanzibaris, cultivated the virtue of sobriety, while the Wasakuma seemed somewhat deficient in muscle and stamina. We were fortunate in securing experienced chiefs; since the head man Bedoe-bin-Ambari had served on two expeditions under Mr. Joseph Thomson, and one with Mr. H. H. Johnston, while Hamadi accompanied Mr. Stanley on one of his earlier travels. The former turned out a rather pronounced malingerer, but the latter possessed all the best qualities of a British non-commissioned officer.

On Saturday the 27th all was ready, and we started from Zanzibar at 3 p.m., Captain Stairs remaining behind to complete the business arrangements. It was a grand sight to see the porters marched down to the harbour from Messrs. Smith and Mackenzie's store. They went in detachments of fourteen or fifteen; one hand grasping a long pole, the other free so that their friends in the crowd could give them presents, while they in return could bestow some of the three months' pay upon sweethearts or wives. There were many partings, but in no case, so far as I could see, was any depth of feeling displayed. Indeed the Zanzibari is seldom bothered with the fine shades of sentiment. With little trouble the men were packed into two dhows, I being in charge of one, and M. de Bonchamps following in the other. The south-west monsoon blew freshly, and the boat with her large lateen sail, slipped through the water at a spanking pace. In fact no single incident occurred to mar the feeling of pleasurable excitement inseparable from a plunge into the unknown. I sat on the after-deck, surrounded by my goods and chattels, with Abdullah by my side. The busy crew hurried about the boat, while the porters, absolutely reckless of the morrow, were enjoying themselves to their hearts' content. Some were munching sugar-cane, others chewing oranges, and all chattering and laughing with genuine abandonment. My ignorance of Swahili caused the conversations to be for the most part unintelligible; still the differences of race and character formed a most interesting study. We sighted Bagamoyo at 5.40 p.m., and dropped anchor about 7 p.m., some three-quarters of a mile from the shore. Darkness came on: I fared sumptuously of fowl and ham, washed down by claret—delicacies from which Abdullah, as a Mohammedan, was compelled to abstain—and turning in slept like the dead throughout the night, though the noise on board must have been terrific.

Next day Bagamoyo, which is hidden from the sea by sandhills, proved to be a decidedly squalid looking town, consisting of a few straggling streets, in which the houses are for the most part mere clay huts, with a stone building here and there. It is ruled by the German officers with a rod of iron, and not without reason, since the moral character of the population lacks honesty and sobriety. No nigger is allowed to be abroad after dark, and each Hindu merchant is compelled to show a light before his house. The landing of the porters took some time, as the dhows could not be beached, and they had to be conveyed ashore in' small boats. Then they were marched up to a *shamba*, or garden containing a barn, provided by the agent, and we fondly imagined that our labour was over for the day. But no such luck, for in half an hour's time they were wandering all over the town, and four miscreants had engaged in a wordy warfare with a poor old Wanyamwesi. He declared they had stolen his goat; they swore by Allah that the beast had been legally purchased for three and a half rupees. Their unanimity of asseveration sounded most suspicious, and the roll-call revealed fresh traits of the Zanzibari character. Thanks to my ignorance of Swahili, several pagazi presented themselves at least twice for their pay, and when taxed with the offence, took refuge in a number of aliases that a London pickpocket would have envied. The operation was protracted over some three hours, and my small stock of patience threatened bankruptcy. At last the gay impostors were safely housed in a hut some hundred and fifty feet long by thirty-five feet wide, and sentinels placed round, in case the Evil One tempted them to desert in the night. In order to effect this lodgement, they evicted a caravan of Wanyamwesi, which had come down to the coast with hoards of ivory. The poor fellows picked up their "duds" and departed in most lamblike fashion before our truculent Zanzibaris. Those warriors, however, being full of meat and impudence, laid hands upon some of these humble pedlars, and compelled them to construct bedsteads made, on the usual pattern, of palm leaves overlaid with cocoanut fibre. The Marquis de Bonchamps and I dined at the hotel, and slept the sleep of the just.

On the 29th, Captain Bodson arrived with his contingent from Dar-es-Salaam, and our commander put in an appearance on the 2nd of July. He at once began to make preparations for the departure on the following Saturday (the 4th), though Bodson and Bonchamps both declared that we should never be ready in time. However, by dint of hard work, the loads were worked, and conveyed to the camp outside the town; the rifles were distributed to the askari (soldiers), who played with them like children with a new rattle. As may well be imagined, there was little time for sight-seeing or enjoyment. Still, we dined with the German officers, who were extremely hospitable, and gave us every possible assistance. In the absence of Baron von Soden, Lieutenant von Schmit took care that our goods were not detained by the customhouse officials, and gave us letters of introduction to the commandants of Mpwapwa and Tabora.

Bonchamps and I also went to the French mission, and were most kindly received by the Father Superior. It has been founded some twenty-six years and seems a most excellent institution. The boys are taught some trade, or learn gardening or farming. They have numerous engineering sheds and workshops, while the girls are instructed by the nuns in a school close by. We went over the extensive plantations of vanilla, coffee, and asparagus, and saw vast groves of cocoanut trees which flourish upon ground which was formerly a barren waste. Altogether we were much impressed by the method and energy of those worthy men.

Incidentally we made some interesting acquaintances during our stay at Bagamoyo. The German sergeant-major introduced me to Miss Panda, a daughter of Emin Pasha's by an Abyssinian mother. I found her a dark and handsome child about eight years old, very self-possessed, and wearing an English sailor hat at a becoming angle. We also became great friends with Captain Jacques of the Belgian Anti-Slavery Society, and his staff of three young officers. They were preparing to march in our rear to Lake Tanganyika, and I may mention by anticipation that we met them again at Tabora and Karema. Yet another visitor presented himself in unconventional fashion, by kicking at the hotel door late at night, and shouting strange oaths in a broad Irish brogue. He had dined, and appeared undecided between pugilism and excessive affection. With some difficulty he explained that he was Mr. Stokes, and had just come down from the Albert Nyanza. We at once recognized his name as that of a famous trader, who was formerly a lay missionary, but has since joined the German service. He has married the daughter of a Wanyamwesi chief, and is much respected throughout the lakes district. Indeed, a nigger has but to announce himself as "a child of Stokes" to be sure of entertainment for the night and a present of cloth to help him on his journey. He was then, of course, on pleasure bent, and as he insisted on grasping the hand of Captain Stairs, the latter had to be routed out of bed. In the confusion of the moment, he put on the Marquis's boots, a mistake which naturally produced fresh complications. After a desultory conversation, the great man departed at 1 a.m., and we were able to snatch a few hours' rest before turning our backs on Bagamoyo.

Chapter III

Usagara and Mpwapwa

We leave Bagamoyo—A typical march—An encampment—The traveller's evenings—Drawbacks to enjoyment—Tippoo Tib—The Makata swamp—Bushiri's fate—An ivory caravan—Usagara—Its possibilities and present condition—Fever—The French mission at Mrogro—The English missionaries—Our porters on the loot—Mamboya and its sultan—Among the mountains—Mpwapwa—A fire in camp—The Wahéhé—Water at last—News of Captain Jacques.

SOME three hours' work had to be put in next morning before we could get fairly under way. At last the start was effected, amidst a great display of enthusiasm from the porters, who yelled at the tops of their voices. When we got into camp, a more elaborate performance took place after dinner. The men marched in a body to Captain Stairs' tent, singing an impromptu and very inharmonious song. Its argument was somewhat as follows: "We will follow the great white chief throughout the world. We will fight well, defeating all his enemies. Neither meat nor drink shall fail; many wives shall fall to our lot. Our labours over; we shall return to Zanzibar with much money." Captain Stairs scattered some small change among the crowd, and. after a scramble, the proceedings came to an end.

As one day telleth another in African travel, I may as well describe a typical march once for all. The drum beats at half-past five a.m.; the loads are distributed, and on the strike of six the men fall in. The askari, or soldiers, lift the burdens, some sixty or seventy pounds in weight, to the porters' heads. (The askari, I may mention, is of superior class to the pagazi, and receives a higher wage.) The commanding officer gives the signal, and the tramp begins. The long column winds out of camp in single file, since the native roads will not permit of two men abreast. In fact, the highways of Africa can best be compared to remarkably sinuous sheep tracks barely a foot wide, and running like ruts through the forest and plain. They have ridges in the middle, on either side of which you must plant your feet. As the black walks perfectly straight, whereas the European turns out his toes, the latter constantly trips against the edges until he gets used to the new conditions. These paths are, of course, centuries old, and their apparently meaningless wanderings are due to fallen trees and other obstacles which have long since perished.

As they draw near a village or another caravan, the men begin to shout and sing, and the drummer to ply his sticks. Imagine yourself among the curious crowd at the entrance of a township, as the multitude approaches along the narrow track, trodden smooth by immemorial generations. First come six soldiers, then the guide, next a chief, Captain Stairs or Captain Bodson, another chief, the drummer, then the long string of porters. The last tramp steadily forward, their arms swinging like pendulums, except when a hand is raised to steady the load for a moment or two. Three-fourths of the distance down the line come the sections of the boats, of which I was in charge, until promoted by Captain Stairs to take my turn with the rear- guard. The white men are distributed along the column to keep a look out against thieving or skulking, and to make the men take close order, if gaps have occurred during a progress through wooded or broken country. Last, but not least, comes the rear-guard, consisting of six askari, two chiefs, and a white man. Their task consists in guarding against attack—always most imminent from that quarter—and in picking up the stragglers as they hide in the bush, or simulate exhaustion by the roadside. It is tedious and exasperating work, nor can the rear-guard reckon on getting into camp until two hours after the main body.

The march generally lasts until midday, seldom later, when the distance covered will have been some eight or ten miles, with a halt for half an hour at 9.30 a.m. At first we were content with six, as the men were out of condition, and suffered from stiffness and blistered feet. The spot selected for the camp depends mostly upon the proximity of water; when it has been chosen, the white men's tents are pitched in a triangle, and as the porters come in, they heap the loads in front of each. The Zanzibaris' tortoise tents form a circle round the officer's quarters. But before many days canvas is discarded in favour of a grass hut, which can be constructed in a very few minutes, and as readily abandoned. Thus the outer and inner lines of defence comprise, the first, the circuit of the camp, the second, the space between the loads. My cook bestirs himself over my lunch, while the Zanzibaris are boiling *ugali* (flour and water), the mess which, eked out with an occasional piece of goat's flesh, forms their staple diet. This paste, which is prepared in brass or tin pots, is eaten in messes of from six to ten, and they get a similar meal at night. Meanwhile an askari or two have been sent into the neighbouring villages to see if fowls or eggs are purchasable. The medium of exchange consists in so many "hands" of cloth (as measured from the elbow to the finger-tips), and a nigger understands as thoroughly how to drive a profitable bargain as any "Sheeny" in Petticoat Lane. Indeed, the manner in which prices rise in a brisk market would turn the British coster bilious with envy. The inner man refreshed, I go forth in search of game, provided the country is reported to be safe, and there are no bad cases to detain me in camp. Sport or no sport, I am supposed to have returned safely by 6 p.m. when the sun goes down. Then comes dinner, a chat and smoke with a white man, or a talk with one of the chiefs. Sometimes, while passing by one of the men's fires, I could hear my moral character and personal appearance being criticised with considerable freedom; or, while sitting still in front of my tent, I might listen to Abdullah and my other boys exchanging confessions of past transgression. One would say, "I stole some cloth from the doctari yesterday," and the other would reply, "You will get beaten, if he discovers you." Of course I never dreamt of taking advantage of these unintended confidences, except by way of precaution against similar peccadilloes. As a rule I felt too tired to read, besides, my library was of necessity limited, and was glad enough to turn in at 9 or 9.30 p.m., after posting up my diary.

Such is the ordinary routine of African travel. It sounds pleasant enough, but entails, nevertheless, a severe strain on the constitution. Under the best of circumstances, the climate, with its rapid changes of temperature, the continued, exertion, the recurrence of the same worries day after day, are calculated to try even the most robust and phlegmatic personalities. At a pinch, you have to undergo fever and dysentery, want of water, and dearth of provisions. Even when food abounds, its eternal sameness becomes unutterably distasteful,, and you long in vain for a change from the perpetual goat's flesh and *matamah*, or Kaffir corn. As Mr. Stanley has most aptly remarked, travellers may shirk the recital of the horrors of the road, but no traveller can forget them.

In writing of Mr. Stanley, I am reminded that some two miles from Bagamoyo, we met the notorious slave-dealer, Tippoo Tib. He was on his way to Zanzibar, there to defend his action with the great explorer for the non-fulfilment of the contract to supply porters for the Emin Relief Expedition. The Arab seemed about sixty years of age, is about five feet ten inches in height, has a very good presence, set off by a short grey beard, and strikes you at once as a man of considerable intelligence. He had been ill at Tabora, and the rumour ran in the English papers that he was suffering from paralysis, but he certainly exhibited no signs of brain mischief. We were curious to learn Tippoo Tib's opinion of Mr. Stanley, which he promptly gave, with a bland assumption of disinterested regret. How it was he could not say, but the great white chief had acquired an indifferent reputation throughout Central Africa. His shortcomings on the score of veracity were notorious; he would say, "Yes" to-day, and "No" tomorrow. In fact, Tippoo Tib considered that Mr. Stanley's unpopularity would endanger his life were he to return to the Congo; and even at Zanzibar he might run some risk of assassination. All this was delivered with an air of imperturbable gravity, which heightened its artistic effect. Fortunately our good manners enabled us to restrain our laughter until the Arab's back was fairly turned; then we gave way to an unrestrained enjoyment of the situation.

The first marches were through the Makata swamp, familiar to readers of *Across Africa*, varied by stream, and several untoward events naturally occurred. Our donkeys unshipped us in rapid succession, and my moke nearly disappeared altogether in the bog. The porters floundered about, but showed wonderful ingenuity in keeping their foothold. Near the ferry over the Luvu, we passed the remains of the fort which the Germans garrisoned with 400 men when the Arab Bushiri was threatening Bagamoyo. It appears that when that freebooter was captured, they tried, sentenced, and hanged him within two hours, and then telegraphed to Berlin for instructions. Just think of the feelings of the Aborigines Protection Society if the British East Africa Company was detected in similar practices! We also passed several large caravans, under German command, one numbering 500 souls, and heavily laden with ivory. There were 234 loads—about 60 large tusks, and the rest in bundles containing three or four. In fact, while we were at Bagamoyo, the conversation turned almost entirely upon ivory, and the cultivation of the soil appeared a matter of secondary importance. I need hardly point out how precarious a source of wealth the former must prove.

Then we began to ascend from the sea-level, journeying through the country of Usagara. The scenery was most enchanting, reminding one not a little of parts of Hampshire and Devonshire. We passed through a succession of groves and glades, varied by the primeval forest. The narrow roadway, barely a foot wide, meandered through dense hedges, or jungle some six feet high. The timber was exceptionally fine, most of the trees averaging two feet in diameter. Sometimes we beheld specimens of that curious vegetation, the baobab tree, with its huge trunk, enormous branches, and twigs some two or three inches in circumference. The comical ugliness of this strange growth is relieved by a beautiful white flower, and it bears a fruit like a stout cucumber. From time to time some magnificent *bombacs* (cotton trees), were seen dominating their brethren, with stems shooting up straight as an arrow for about ninety feet, and then expanding into a mass of foliage. The strychnine bush also flourished in great abundance. Away to our left loomed the mighty Makessi, or "Lion of Mountains", bearing due south, and lending dignity to a panorama that would otherwise have aspired merely to prettiness.

I see no reason why the Usagara country should not become in the course of years a source of wealth to the German empire. The soil is rich, and suited to the cultivation of the products of Southern India and Ceylon. Cattle and sheep would thrive on the excellent pasturage, more especially as the tsetse fly does not appear to infest the neighbourhood. Water also exists in abundance, and with a little trouble it could be made drinkable by human beings. The chief requisite for the district's development is a permanent white population which, becoming acclimatized in a generation or two, would thrive where now the European dies. The causes of the fevers that decimate Teutonic immigrants are the heat, bad water-supply, indifferent and undigestible food, and, last but not least, the altered conditions of living. Many of these evils can obviously be alleviated, and with a railway and the influx of capital the territory has every chance of paying its way.

At present Usagara is little better than a waste. Not a head of cattle is to be seen on the vast savannahs, since the natives content themselves with a goat or two, and some very primitive attempts at tillage. They are a miserable set, vegetarians for the most part, and dwelling in round hovels without the usual *boma* or encircling palisade. Their villages, scattered at long intervals over the plain, offered the feeblest resistance to the German occupation. There was indeed an attempt at a battle in 1889 near. a place called Kisema, but the Soudanese and Zulu mercenaries won an almost bloodless victory. Chiefs had since been placed over every village with instructions to fly the German flag, and if this edict is transgressed the misguided headman promptly suffers the extreme penalty of the law.

The nights had now begun to turn extremely cold, and the ensuing heat in the daytime taxed our strength rather severely. Most of the white men had touches of fever, Robinson's being a particularly severe attack, which was actually contracted before he landed. Among the sufferers was Captain Bodson, who insisted for several days that there was nothing whatever the matter with him beyond biliousness. I took his temperature and found it 102.4°. "Oh," said he, "that's nothing. Why on the Congo I had my temperature at 108° and 110° for days together." It was useless to argue that, under those circumstances, he must be constituted very differently from the rest of mankind, and after a plucky attempt to laugh the complaint to scorn, he was forced to surrender at discretion and take quinine.

As the men showed signs of wear and tear, Captain Stairs determined to halt for a day (July the 19th), near the French mission-station of Mrogro. The good fathers sent us an invitation to dinner, of which Bodson, Bonchamps, and I availed ourselves, and we were received with the utmost kindness. This institution was founded in 1882, and burnt down three years later. It has rapidly recovered from that misfortune and soon hopes to be self-supporting. The situation has been chosen with an eye to the picturesque, on the side of a mountain looking due north. For the sake of defence a deep trench surrounds the bungalow, chapel, and school-house; while the native village has been built outside this enclosure. The plantations abound in coffee, sugar-cane, Indian corn, pineapples, five different kinds of bananas, and fruits of all descriptions. Next day Bodson and the Marquis, who had slept at the mission, returned laden with vegetables and loaves. The latter provender was most acceptable, since, owing to the incompetency of our cooks, we had not tasted bread since leaving Bagamoyo.

The difficulties of the country increased as we neared Mamboya, some of the gradients being decidedly severe. On the 26th, we fell in with the English missionaries Messrs. Ashe, Hubbard, Collins, and Dr. Wright on their way to Uganda where, as the world knows, they underwent strange experiences. One of their number, Mr. Greaves, had been compelled to return to the coast, as he was suffering from a severe attack of dysentery. We had the pleasure of travelling in their company for several days, finally bidding them farewell on the 31st, a march beyond Mamboya. Thanks to Mr. Ashe, we were able to make a disagreeable, but, at the same time, useful discovery. He went out shooting and, greatly to his surprise, discovered that every village was deserted and that the natives ran away on being accosted. With some difficulty he caught one black fellow, who explained that the porters of the two caravans had been looting the whole countryside, using threats and sometimes violence. The matter being reported to Captain Stairs, he picked out five of the chief offenders, and flogged them soundly, to the vast improvement of their own and their comrades' morals.

We had to make a forced march to Mamboya through very trying country. Some of the slopes were nearly perpendicular, though at one point our labours were relieved by a natural viaduct some twenty yards wide and three hundred feet deep, which stretched from hill to hill. About two miles from Mamboya, the name given not to a village but to a gorge between two mountains, we entered into cultivated country. Fields of *matamah* ten feet high alternated with beans and sweet potatoes, divided from the road by a well-kept fence. In spite of their industry, the natives (Wasaghara) are, as I have said, a miserable race, very low down in the scale of humanity, and possessing no religious ideas whatever. Their stock of courage seems decidedly limited, and they complained to us bitterly of the exactions of the Germans, who are accused of demanding contributions in kind, to the complete impoverishment of the district. The men who came into camp were indescribably filthy, and the only occasion on which water touched their person was when it rained or a river had to be crossed. Some of them wore their hair long, and had trained it over an animal's bladder placed on the crown of the head. This extraordinary chignon was smeared with red clay and fat, the whole erection forming a sufficiently loathsome spectacle.

Next morning I was favoured with a visit from the Sultan of Mamboya, whose village lay just below our camp. He announced himself as Wanamoka by name, and complained of severe fits of ague. I asked him his age, and he said two months—in reality he was at least sixty years old—and his remaining statements were of the vaguest, particularly upon matters of faith. Upon two points only would he commit himself the number of his family—ten wives, four sons, and six daughters— and his friendship for white men. The latter assertion he repeated several times with rising emphasis. The unprejudiced have described him, nevertheless, as an unprincipled old scoundrel, who is ready on all occasions to sell himself to the highest bidder. I gave him some medicine; he bowed low, and departed.

The scenery had now become Alpine, and some of the loftier peaks would have delighted the heart of Mr. Whymper. Much of the stone is white marble; and, if it could be conveyed to the coast, would be a source of considerable profit. To a heavily laden caravan, however, the inclines, varied by dry river-beds, were almost heart-breaking, and the pagazi were severely distressed at the end of each march. Those carrying the sections of the boats had a most arduous experience; as, in addition to the rocks, the road was frequently obstructed by fallen trees. The poor fellows suffered severely from the cold, and at night time storms of wind and sand arose, which blew for several hours, and threatened to overturn the tents. Indeed, Robinson's tabernacle was actually upset while he was having a bath. It is not too much to say that we were all pretty well beat when, on the 4th of August, after a terrific descent, down which the porters plunged with absolute recklessness of life and limb, the mountains suddenly opened and disclosed the plain of Mpwapwa.

Imagine a gently undulating space, surrounded by mountains and covered with fields of *matamah* and sweet potatoes. Due south lies a large lake, shining pleasantly in the sunshine, about three miles away. Very few cattle are to be seen, for the deadly foot-and-mouth disease has swept through the valley and carried off some six thousand head. Some twenty villages are dotted over the plain, containing about four hundred inhabitants. They are miserably poor, owing to the destruction of their beasts. In other respects Mpwapwa is hardly a desirable habitation, since dysentery and pneumonia abound, though it is situated some two thousand four hundred feet above the sea. We encamped within half a mile of the German fort, which stands on a knoll in the centre of the open. it is strongly built, and was then garrisoned by a contingent of fifty Soudanese and Zulus, under Herr von Alssous. They were a fine body of men, especially the Zulus, and their commandant appeared an excellent specimen of the German soldier. His was no child's play, since he had to make some two expeditions a month against the warlike chiefs of the neighbourhood. Next day he proposed to set out on the chastisement of a potentate who had killed one of his men; and the afternoon was accordingly spent in rifle practice with Captain Bodson and the Marquis de Bonchamps, though they both beat him. Just above our camp was another fort, now dismantled, which had been built some two and a half years previously by an officer of the German East Africa Company. Six months afterwards the poor chap's throat was cut by the Arabs. In the afternoon Captain Stairs paid a visit to the English mission, about two miles away, and came back full of its praises. I was unfortunately detained in camp by a touch of fever, and so was unable to accompany him.

While travelling across the plain by easy stages, we were joined by a large caravan of Wanyamwesi, who travelled in our rear for protection until we reached Tabora. We then entered upon a barren tract of land upon which little appeared to flourish, in the shape either of game or vegetation. The evening of the 6th witnessed a conflagration in camp, the porters having built one of their fires close to fine old tree which was fast decaying into touch-wood. After a prodigious amount of yelling and excitement the mischief was got under. The next five-and-twenty hours were passed without any water to drink, and the men appeared utterly spent. We were passing, moreover, through dangerous country, as the Wahéhé away to the south exist by professional brigandage, robbing the more peaceful tribes and waylaying weak caravans. They had already accounted for one German expedition, and in the following year, as my readers will doubtless remember, they made a shocking example of that commanded by Lieutenant Zelewski. Fortunately they considered us too strong for attack, and the only sign of their prowess was the body of a dead nigger by the roadside. Captain Stairs told me that it lay within a short distance of the spot on which Dr. Parke shot two of the Wahéhé, when he came down-country in Mr. Stanley's rear-guard. Occasionally we saw small bands of these barbarians, seldom numbering more than four or five. They were tall, spare and wiry-looking men, who could have rendered excellent account of themselves, though armed, for the most part, with bows and arrows. Remarkably enough, though extremely dangerous to strangers, they seldom molest those from whom they have received a kindness. The

French fathers regard them with little apprehension, and go in and out of the villages with perfect safety. On the 8th the men could scarcely crawl, and Captain Bodson, who was in charge of the rear-guard, had great difficulty in collecting the stragglers. At last, about nine o'clock, a shout was raised from the first division of "Water! water!" The pagazi instantly threw down their loads and rushed for the green and stagnant pool, fighting and squalling like fiends. The Wanyamwesi caravan came up at the same moment, and some hundreds of men were tumbling and struggling in the pond. Though it was soon churned into liquid mud, they sat therein and bathed themselves with every sign of enjoyment.

That evening a runner came in with a letter from the commandant of Mpwapwa. It announced the arrival of Captain Jacques after a most tedious and unpleasant march. His men seemed to have become completely disorganized, and instead of paying the natives, had looted every village on the road. We naturally hoped that so disreputable a band would not catch us up, as their misdeeds must inevitably affect our reputation and breed trouble; but in justice to Captain Jacques I should say that the story was afterwards shown to have been decidedly overcoloured. I may mention that the discipline throughout our caravan was now excellent, Captain Stairs' division, in particular, starting each morning with the punctuality of clock-work, and keeping admirable order throughout the stage.

Chapter IV

Ugogo and Unyamyembe

Ugogo—Scarcity of water—Nakedness of the land—The Wagogo—Their weapons and dress—The women—The Wanyamwesi caravans—Mount Kilimandini—The Arab's sanctum—A matrimonial dispute—Mahara—We enter Unyanyembe—The Wanyamwesi—Their caravans—Mwamba's village—My interview with the sultan—Zanzibari improvidence—Two water systems—A fertile district—Alarm in camp—Arrival of Captain Jacques—Makangi's further exploits.

WE were now crossing a level plateau, having left the mountains in our rear. This country of Ugogo is about a hundred miles square. For several days we marched on loose sandy soil varied by stretches of jungle. To our right lay a splendid range of hills about five miles off, and on the 9th we passed a most curious heap of large rocks about one hundred and fifty feet high, and apparently of a formation different from the surrounding minerals. They are apparently those described by Commander Cameron in his book *Across Africa*. On the whole the actual travelling wearied the men considerably less than the journey from Mamboya to Mpwapwa. Still the scarcity of provisions and want of water tried the pagazis' strength severely, and my daily sick-list began to assume portentous lengths. There was every probability that loads would be considerably in excess of porters by the time we reached Tabora; a predicament the more to be dreaded because the contingent engaged at Mamboya, having fulfilled its contract, insisted on returning home. On the 12th, and again on the 13th, we had two very severe marches, as on getting into camp we found that the wells were insufficient to satisfy the caravan and the Wanyamwesi hangers-on. I may mention that Ugogo has very little surface-water in the dry season, The fluid is obtained by digging in the hollows or else in pits constructed to catch the rain, while here and there a well is to be found. As the summer passes into autumn, these supplies become abominably nauseous, their disagreeable qualities being intensified by the salt in the ground.

Ugogo, when we made its acquaintance, was suffering from an acute attack of agricultural depression. In prosperous seasons the natives own large herds of cows, which the males of the tribe tend in rotation. But the numerous carcases of cattle lying about the plain testified to the ravages of the ubiquitous foot-and-mouth disease, and even the goats appeared to have been destroyed by a similar epidemic. No fowls were obtainable, even at the most exorbitant prices, and though eggs were sold, they had greatly deteriorated from their pristine freshness. Thanks to Abdullah's preternatural acuteness in detecting these impostures, I escaped certain experiences upon which the Marquis and Captain Bodson commented in very forcible language. By way of compensation we had some good duck shooting near the bed of the Sebubu; but our feelings were much tantalized by the news that big game, though invisible, was close at hand, including numerous lions. Indeed the maned or hunting sort is said to abound in the desert stretches of Ugogo, but we did not get so much as a shot.

The Wagogo are thick upon the soil in comparison with the natives of Usagara, and both their villages and themselves belong to a higher order of society. The former, instead of miserable clusters of beehive-shaped hovels, are composed of rows of stoutly built rectangular huts, made of wooden frame-works wattled with clay, and thatched with *matamah* straw. These houses are arranged in square or oblong fashion, so that the back wall of each, strengthened by a thick palisade, forms part of the *boma*, or outer defence, the inner pace being about fifty yards square. Such is a Wagogo *tembé*, or Village, and its inhabitants have all the characteristics of a brave and warlike nation. They profess to hold the Arab in great contempt, indeed, the sheikhs have more than once attempted to invade the country without success. The people of whom they stand in most awe are the Masai, a tribe living partly in German and partly in British territory. Want of water for their flocks generally drives the latter south in summer time; a collision occurs at the wells, and the Wagogo generally get worsted. But as yet they have not been inspired with any marked reverence for the European. Unlike the Wasaghara they flocked fearlessly into camp, examined our belongings with some freedom, and generally behaved as if the place was their own. I could see that they would not have thought twice about an attack, had we been a weak caravan. Indeed, Captain Stairs, on passing the village of the powerful chief Makangi, who declined to visit us on the score of age and blindness, thought it advisable to cultivate the potentate's good graces by a payment of *mhongo*, or tribute, and I shall show that Captain Jacques' experiences proved the procedure to be most advisable. On the march we were extremely careful to prevent gaps in the line, and to keep a sharp eye on stragglers. Nevertheless, one unfortunate porter, who was suffering from fever, eluded the vigilance of the rear-guard as he crouched in the bush. We sent out a body of askaris to bring on, but as they could discover no traces of the man or his load, he had probably been converted into meat for jackals, together with several more deliberate deserters. As an excuse for the Wagogo, I may mention that the Arabs seldom give their porters any *posho*, or rations, after Mpwapwa. The poor devils are, in consequence, forced to rob the villages, and the country-side becomes inconveniently "hot."

Indeed, taken all round, the Wagogo warrior is no bad specimen of humanity. He exhibits in a marked degree the physical advantages of the flesh-eater over the vegetarian; for some of the men, whose measurements I took, showed splendid development, particularly about the chest and shoulders. Of intellect he can make but little boast, at least the braves with whom we conversed did not appear to be gifted with a superfluity of brains. But he is skilled in the use of arms—the bow, the double-edged knife, and the club. The most characteristic weapon of the race, however, is a spear some five feet ten inches long. The head, measuring about ten inches, is set in wood which in turn fits into a shaft of iron. Its edge has the sharpness of a penknife, and is frequently used in a similar fashion. This missile is hurled by a flick of the wrist with extraordinary dexterity; for Instance, a marksman can bring down a particular bunch of fruit from a high tree. In person the Wagogo are hardly nice, since they smear themselves with red clay and oil, which arrangement is held to necessitate a careful disregard of the matutinal tub. Moreover they twist their hair into the most Singular shapes, and carry brass earrings or even Pieces of wood in the lobe of the ear, which descends almost to the shoulder They also affect bracelets and anklets. Yet, in spite of this strange bedizenment, they are a well-featured and not uncomely race.

The young women and girls are distinctly handsome, as niggers go, and cultivate the graces of beauty unadorned. Instead of affecting a cloth extending from the breast to below the knee, as their more modest sisters of Usagara, a scanty garment round the waist suffices for their attire. By way of compensation, the hair is dressed with small brass balls made of twisted wire, upon which the sun plays with pleasing effect. Indeed, the Wagogo damsel assumes all the airs of an enchantress during the short season of her comeliness. As with most African tribes, this ceases with the twentieth year, and a female of thirty has degenerated into a repulsive crone. They seldom live later than sixty, and death must happen as a merciful release, since the thrifty community turns them out to starve when they can drudge no more. The equality of the sexes by no means obtains as an article of faith among the Wagogo. Yet another Wanyamwesi caravan joined us on the 17th, bringing up our total strength to some 2200 men. The arrangement was greatly to the new-comers' advantage, as they had previously lost six loads, through the bearers being cut off by the Wagogo. To us, however, the addition of numerical strength hardly brought corresponding advantages. Before long an askari was detected by one of the *Nyamparas* (chiefs) in the act of selling his rifle to a Wanyamwesi tempter, and was incontinently flogged for the misdemeanour. Moreover, the presence of so large a multitude naturally caused a dearth of provisions, and we were still pursued by apprehensions of Captain Jacques and his band, now only two marches in our rear. Whenever we arrived at a well, Captain Stairs stationed askaris round it until our men were satisfied, otherwise the Wanyamwesi would not have left a drop. Still there were compensations, notably on the 20th when we ascended Mount Kilimandini. All the morning we had tramped across a plain divided about halfway by a low range of hills. Suddenly we began to climb a steep pass which tried the porters cruelly, particularly those in charge of the boats. At last we reached the top and encamped within some fifty yards of the brow. I turned and looked back upon the caravans. They appeared as a huge serpent winding up the mountain side and stretching for some five miles along the valley. The spectacle provoked feelings of the liveliest enjoyment and hardly less impressive was the sight of our porters drawn up in single file across the summit's edge, with the askaris on either flank to prevent the Wanyamwesi from getting ahead. They resembled a large army in battle array, calmly awaiting the foe.

I had occasion to visit one of the Wanyamwesi camps, as some of its inmates were sick. These curious people do not carry tents, but build instead little huts of boughs stacked like rifles in a barrack yard and covered with stalks of *matamah*. These tabernacles last for many months, and are regarded as common property which each expedition is free to occupy in succession. The women accompany the *safari* in numbers of fifty or sixty, and the harem of the Arab chief is formed in a very primitive fashion. A canvas fence, similar to those erected at English race-meetings for purposes of "roll, bowl, or pitch" at the cocoanuts, encloses the sanctum. Within this space stands the tent, so that the dames and their lord need fear no interruption of the pleasures of seclusion. It is perhaps hardly necessary to say that the Arabs have acquired a great ascendancy over the Wanyamwesi, and are rapidly transforming the national characteristics. Indeed most of the caravans we passed on the road were commanded by these sons of the desert, who seemed to exercise a fairly humane authority.

In one rather amusing instance the Arab even erred on the side of leniency. We had just encamped, when a Wanyamwesi lady appeared in a mighty quandary, followed by a harassed-looking man. It appeared that the pair had somehow come to blows, that the woman had appealed to her master, who professed inability to decide so complicated a problem. Accordingly she came to lay her grievances before the Great White Chief; and this she did with amazing volubility. The scene was amusingly reminiscent of an East End row; the same gestures, the same shrill invective on the part of the female, the same surly and brief rejoinders from the superior sex. Captain Stairs heard both sides with exemplary patience, and then in a tone of paternal dignity recommended mutual forgiveness and forgetfulness. Unfortunately the lady was unable to resist the temptation of the last word, and directly they regained their camp the hubbub began afresh. Accordingly, Captain Stairs sent a message to the perplexed Arab that, diplomacy having failed, the only remaining remedy was coercion. How far his advice was followed we never heard, but a profound peace came over that encampment after the arrival of his messenger.

Two days (August 20th and 21st) were spent at Mahara, so as to rest the men and hire porters in lieu of those about to regain their native Mamboya. The place is generally considered to mark the boundary between Ugogo and Unyanyembe, but so greatly are the peoples confounded that the correct demarcation of the two would be no easy matter. For instance, some five marches from Mahara lies a settlement of Wanyanwesi, who, having been exiled from their own country for some treasonable act, were granted asylum by the tolerant Wagogo. Again we came across a second village of this semi-nomadic race, in the midst of a waste which they were engaged in reclaiming, thanks to the discovery of an excellent stream of water. For several days we passed through *pori*, or desert, upon which nothing grew beyond small resinous shrubs. The water, however, was excellent, and a most agreeable change from the liquid mud supplied by the Wagogo. Curiously enough, not a single nigger showed himself, though they were doubtless lurking in the bush on the look out for a stray porter.

At length we attained a more populated region, and were at once struck by the peaceful appearance of the inhabitants as compared with the Wagogo. Their physique is decidedly inferior, and they do not affect the same bravery of apparel, the distinguishing marks of the race being the filing of a triangular notch in the front teeth, and tattooed lines down the centre of the forehead and on each temple. The women wear much more voluminous attire than their sisters of Wagogo, being clothed from the breast to below the knee. Their manners, unfortunately, do not correspond to this refreshing sense of propriety; on the contrary, they are alarmingly free and easy. As we passed each village our porters (many of whom were themselves Wanyamwesi) used to shout out very broad remarks to the assembled matrons, and they certainly showed no reluctance to reply in kind. In the afternoon the camp was always full of villagers, who seemed much interested in everything they saw, particularly the sections of the boats. Their remarks showed distinct intelligence; in fact, the Wanyamwesi is far more a man of the world than the Wagogo.

Time was when the race were good fighters as well; indeed, their king Mirambo, held his own during the seventies against the Arabs, raiding the settlements and carrying off the cattle. However, with his death and the accession of a young son, the military prowess of Unyanyembe has declined. The Arabs rule the roost, and smuggle guns and ammunition galore, without any interference from the

Germans. The energies of the people are, accordingly, absorbed in travel, and they trade in ivory, copper wire, salt, honey, and so forth, over the whole of Central Africa, frequently journeying in large caravans, and being absent from home for two years or more. These expeditions are generally commanded by Arabs, in which case they probably consist for the most part of slaves. But very frequently voluntary associations are formed every spring, a drummer beating up recruits from village to village, which journey down to the coast or into the interior. Some of the Wanyamwesi are very clever smiths, therefore the Wagogo kidnap them to fashion spears and other weapons of war. I may mention that though many of our pagazi were passing through their native homesteads, with the terrors of an unknown land before them, not a man deserted nor made away with his load. Their less adventurous fellow-countrymen were actuated by more questionable motives in the matter of commerce. Out of twelve eggs purchased from Wamba's *tembé* (village), every one proved a "wrong un"; and these dishonest merchants expressed surprise and indignation, when I declined to pay for the impostures.

On the afternoon of the 27th, I visited Mwamba, the king of the district, as one of his wives was badly afflicted with small-pox. His village was the largest we had entered since leaving the coast. The outer *boma* consisted of a dense hedge of euphorbia, constructed in a circle. Thirty paces further on I entered a thick palisade, within which were the flat-roofed and earth-covered huts of the common people. Yet a third enclosure, rectangular in form, separated the houses of the monarch and his wives from the vulgar herd. Each lady—there were twenty-five in all—owned a separate residence, and Mwamba inhabited a large conical hut in their midst. All over the village were placed stakes, surmounted by lions' skulls as symbols, doubtless, of sovereignty. I should mention that without the euphorbia hedge, there was a settlement of Watusi. This tribe of herdsmen is totally distinct from the Wanyamwesi, and its home lies on the road to Ujiji. I imagine that that they must have been made prisoners of war in some campaign of Mwamba's; and lived, in consequence, a life of helotry as the personal property of the king.

Mwamba proved to be a little man, about five feet two inches in height, and sixty years of age. He bore a very indifferent reputation for cruelty and rapacity, but his behaviour to me was distinctly courteous and agreeable. My numerous questions were answered with promptitude and discrimination. He seemed very proud of his army, some two hundred men armed with muzzle-loaders, and told me that the population of the village comprised five hundred males, four hundred women, and an uncounted number of children. His three huge war-drums were evidently a source of royal gratification. They were beaten to assemble the braves for battle, or to resist attack, and could be heard for an immense distance. Then we passed his domestic paraphernalia under review; notably the huge bins of wattles and mud, in which he stored his corn. Most of Mwamba's furniture had been imported from Zanzibar, for instance the bedsteads, which replaced the ordinary wooden pillow. Also the doors and window-frames of his house were of Zanzibari workmanship. But the greatest treasure was reserved for the last, when, with an air of great importance, he showed me a piece of looking-glass hanging against a wall. I expressed the utmost admiration for this inestimable prize, and the king evidently considered me a person of insight and refinement.

My patient was in a terrible state, more especially as the wise man of the village could devise no more efficacious cure than some string tied round the head as a charm. I asked Mwamba if the tribe knew of any medicines. He said, "No, merely a root which we boil and use as a purgative," and with that answer he appeared entirely satisfied. Equally complacent was his confession of a somewhat negative creed. "Did he believe in a God?" "No." "Had he faith in a hereafter?" "No." "Were his people equally limited in their religious views?" "Yes." I could not help thinking that this agnosticism was assumed to baffle the stranger, since the Wanyamwesi in our caravan used to worship the moon, in whose honour they were wont to blaze off their rifles, greatly to the disturbance of the camp. Moreover, in the fields of Unyanyembe, as in other parts of Africa, you sometimes see little huts containing meat and, drink for the god of the harvest, a custom evidently pointing to the existence of some form of religion. Similarly small models of houses are set up to attract the rain.

The marches, after leaving Mwamba's, were through *pori*, and the men suffered terribly from want of water. In spite of repeated warnings, at least two-thirds persisted in starting with unfilled gourds, and endured torments in consequence. The Wanyamwesi caravans were far more provident, and brought supplies into camp every evening, which they sold at famine prices. On the 30th, while I was in command of the rear-guard the pagazi literally stormed a village in search of the precious liquid, but with the aid of the inhabitants we managed to get them put into the road. Next night, my donkey-boy, Abdullah-Mizé, rode ahead of the camp and returned two hours later with a most welcome flask full. This was a decidedly plucky feat, as very few Zanzibaris will face the dangers of the bush after sunset. Most of the men had to sleep without a drop or bit of food, and on the morrow another boy, Mizé-bin-Pharo, nearly died. The hare-brained youngster had hypothecated his rations, and had been compelled to exist for days upon such scraps as he could pick up. Our march of fifteen miles—the longest stage throughout the expedition—along a glaring sandy road, nearly finished off many of the porters, and the sick list assumed the most formidable proportions.

On the 1st of September we crossed a low range of hills dividing the water-system of East Africa from that of Tanganyika and the Lualaba, with its continuation, the Congo. The eminence stands 3,690 feet above the sea level, and is situated 475 miles from the coast. From that point everything began to improve; water was found in abundance, and the exchange from the *matamah* of Ugogo to Indian corn greatly benefited the men's health. The chiefs bought bullocks and sold the meat to the rank and file, the camp being converted into a regular *soko* (fair), of gesticulating and bawling hucksters. Moreover a Wanyamwesi woman on her travels brought news that all was right at Karema, whence we proposed to cross Tanganyika. This intelligence greatly cheered us, as we had heard that the place had been abandoned by the white men and occupied by Rumaliza's Arabs. On the 5th we actually beheld grass for the first time since the beginning of August, and the hills were clothed with trees to their very summits.

Curiously enough this fertile district appeared a mere *pori*, wholly destitute of villages. It was reported, besides, to be infested by *ruga-ruga*, or brigands, from Tabora, who waylay stray porters, cut their throats, and disappear with their loads. We were ready to give these gentlemen a warm reception, but none appeared, though on the night of the 5th there was an alarm of attack. On all sides of the camp, fire suddenly emerged from the bush, and the appearances favoured a design to rush the caravan in the consequent confusion. Captain Stairs promptly fell in the askaris, and sent Captain Bodson to reconnoitre on the west. The latter returned, after about half an hour, with two natives, who explained that the bush had been set aflame, so that the guinea-fowl might become stifled with the smoke and then be caught. The story seemed more plausible than convincing, and as the firing of the scrub continued, I tried to stalk the offenders with the Nyampara Sadi and an askari, but we returned empty handed. Abdullah carried my gun, and behaved remarkably well, never showing the slightest symptom of fear. After the prisoners had been given a few cuts with the stick and turned out of camp, quietude regained possession of the neighbourhood. Throughout the turmoil, Captain Stairs displayed the greatest coolness, giving his orders in an undertone, so that the Wanyamwesj, encamped around us, had no idea that anything unusual was taking place.

Next day (the 6th), we had barely encamped, when Captain Jacques and his caravan arrived. We were delighted to find them in excellent health, notwithstanding some very arduous experiences, and the pleasure extended to our rank and file. Indeed, several of our Nyamparas celebrated the occasion by getting extremely drunk on *pombé*, and then serenading the Belgian officers with a most inharmonious enthusiasm. One of them, I regret to say, was the valiant Sadi, who evidently felt that the sternest warrior must unbend on occasions. From Captain Jacques we received a most animated account of his march through Ugogo, which resolved itself, practically, into a running fight. Soon after entering the country he lost a porter, who was killed and his load stolen. Near King Makangi's village the column was cut in two by a sudden rush, and six pagazi promptly bit the dust. A rout seemed imminent, but the Captain brought his repeating rifle to bear upon the enemy, who sheered off after losing about ten killed and four wounded. On the following day the Wagogo again menaced the caravan in force, when the Belgians accounted for fifteen and they retired to a respectful distance; though not until one of the officers, having expended his ammunition, was reduced to pointing his empty gun at the dusky spearmen. During the remainder of the afternoon, small detachments of the native army hovered round the camp, but did not venture upon close quarters. In the evening there came a messenger from King Makangi, saying that his warriors would fight no more. Captain Jacques replied that, for his part, the combat had been entirely unprovoked; that he was passing through the country on a purely pacific mission, and had no desire for bloodshed; but that, if wantonly assailed, he should most certainly act in self-defence. In spite of this plain-spoken declaration, Makangi's braves again attacked the caravan near the camp before Kilimindini. This time the Wagogo surprised the rear-guard, and spear a porter, after he had, most gallantly, engaged four of them single-handed. Captain Jacques, however, rallied his askari, and then made play with his repeater with such vigour that the retreat was sounded without further ado. Indeed, throughout the anxious week, the savages seemed to have relied entirely upon paralyzing resistance by their first rush, and when it was stopped, they had little appetite left for a second. Here ended Captain Jacques's deeds of prowess in Ugogo, since the chief of the Kilimandini district at once disclaimed all warlike designs, and even provided the expedition with porters to replace those who had fallen in action. We were able to congratulate the Belgian officers on the extremely creditable manner in which they had extricated their weak caravan, and they, in return, entirely acquitted us of having exasperated the Wagogo, and so caused reprisals. In fact, as I have already shown, the conduct of our men, while marching through that hostile territory, was most exemplary—far more forbearing, in all probability, than that of European soldiers would have been under similar circumstances.

The stories we heard about King Makangi, on reaching Tabora, convinced us that, despite his supposed blindness, the Germans have in him a most formidable antagonist. Within a few weeks he had stopped the mail, and cut up a caravan on its way to the coast with ivory. It appeared that he had annexed one half, Mwamba appropriated the other, and the porters, who survived, straggled back to Tabora in the last stages of destitution. The general opinion among the Europeans was that the Governor, Baron von Soden, would have to reckon with this uncompromising barbarian at an early date; otherwise the main road from the interior must be considered unsafe for any except the strongest expeditions, and his administration would thus be involved in no small amount of discredit.

OMER BODSON

Chapter V

Tabora

Tabora—An Arab house—The town and its inhabitants—A centre of the slave trade—Lieutenant von Siegl—The Wali—Difficulties of the situation—Tippoo Tib's boast—The smuggling of arms and ammunition—Arab diplomacy—Ali-bin-Suleiman—The "baraza"—The Wali's donkey—Herr von Siegl's table-talk—A Wangoni war-dance—A Zanzibari hall—The blind singer—Captain Stairs sets out—My Wangoni patient—M. Vrithoff's illness.—I follow after the caravan.

ON the 9th of September, at 8 a.m., we entered Tabora or Unyanyembe, after marching for some two hours through fields of maize and sweet potatoes. The town consists, strictly speaking, of a collection of villages scattered over a considerable space, and to us was allotted a *tembé** on the extreme west, which had previously been honoured by Tippoo Tib. More than an hour was spent in trudging through the streets, but the animation of the scene amply compensated for the delay. The whole of the population turned out in our honour, and displayed the greatest interest in the caravan and its appurtenances, particularly the sections of the boats. Indeed, we formed, including Captain Jacques' force, and the Wanyamwesj caravans, a sufficiently imposing multitude, some two thousand strong. At length we reached our destination, and while the porters dispersed among the surrounding huts, the staff (Europeans and Nyamparas) occupied a large Arab house, built of sun-dried brick. Rectangular in shape, it comprised a series of low rooms and passages fronting on to a courtyard and protected from the heat by a verandah. The place would have been comfortable enough had it not been for the rats, which had already garrisoned the building in overwhelming

---

* The word *tembé* means both a village and a house, and is used most frequently in the former sense.

numbers. They made alarming inroads on our provisions, and at night time the human intruder was made aware of their presence by playful bites on the toes, or a tail whisking about his cheek.

A walk round the town disclosed a very cheerful prospect, especially after the arid steppes which we had recently traversed. Tabora is situated on a small plateau, which rises from an immense plain stretching to the horizon, where the sky-line is broken by some insignificant hillocks. Its component villages, Arab and Wanyamwesi, are arranged with little attempt at symmetry; and each is surrounded by an enclosure planted with mango, millet, and forth. This apparent disorder is dictated, nevertheless, by policy; since a compact city would be liable to destruction by fire, and the water supply depends upon various isolated wells.

Accordingly, the Arabs have not allowed the natives to build a township like Mwamba's, but keep the various settlements apart; the square houses of the former and conical huts of the latter alternating in picturesque confusion. The population of the whole neighbourhood can only be calculated approximately, because of the constant fluctuations produced by the arrival and departure of caravans. It may, however, be roughly stated at twenty thousand souls, among whom the dominant influence is that of a hundred Arabs hailing from Muscat. Most of these men are very wealthy, one owning the whole of the manioc growth of Tabora, while others have amassed fortunes by the traffic in ivory and slaves. At the moment of our arrival, however, these gentlemen had been severely hit by the foot-and-mouth disease, which had hardly spared a single herd of cattle in the district.

Altogether the morals of Tabora hardly square with European notions of propriety. A considerable section of the community subsists on pure brigandage, notably some disreputable Zanzibaris, whose predatory and murderous instincts entailed their expulsion from the coast several years ago. The Wanyamwesi, too, of this district, bear a very bad character for highway robbery and attacks on caravans. In other respects they cultivate, on a minor scale, the practices of their Arab masters. Guns are abundant, and powder fairly cheap. Accordingly, they find little difficulty in fitting out small expeditions to hunt for slaves and ivory round Lake Tanganyika. This class of merchandise commands a ready market; and on the proceeds of his industry the native can spend the winter at home in a condition of conscientious drunkenness, pending the arrival of the dry season. Tabora, in fact, reeks of slavery, and that commerce is conducted under the thinnest of thin disguises. Indeed, ranks and degrees of servitude have become established; thus the slave of a powerful Arab will frequently own numerous drudges of his own. It is only just to say that the treatment of these human chattels seems very fairly humane, and that *Uncle Tom's Cabin* should be banished from the mind, while the attempt is made to realize Tabora. Still the predominant habits of the community are those of pillage and general lawlessness. Before the German occupation, *mhongo*, or tribute, was exacted to such an arbitrary degree, that many caravans passing through this region of anarchy were absolutely ruined.

Early in 1891, Lieutenant von Siegl, an Austrian officer in the German service, was ordered to advance from Lake Victoria and occupy, if possible, Tabora. He had but a handful of Soudanese, and, on his way, had to fight a series of pitched battles with the Wangoni, a tribe of Zulu origin. After a steady resistance, those gallant warriors were completely defeated; and subsequently the commandant, by a brilliant stroke of genius, enlisted some five and twenty in the German service. With his small army, some eighty-five strong, he drew near Tabora, and entered into communications with the Arabs. So impressed were they by his conquest of the Wangoni, that no opposition was made to the occupation of the town, which was effected in the month of February. Here, then, he encamped with his little company, in the midst of enemies that could easily muster some four thousand rifles, and with very precarious means of communicating with the coast. Under the circumstances, force was out of the question, and Herr von Siegl had recourse to diplomacy. He managed to patch up a *modus vivendi* with the Arabs, whereby his dignity was safeguarded by their disclaimer from trading in slaves and ammunition. He was also fortunate in being able to lay hands upon Seef-bin-Saad, an Arab whose goodwill to Europeans had already been manifested by his rescue of the French missionaries of Kipalapala, during the rebellion of 1888. For three days the Fathers were hidden in his house, while the populace thirsted for their blood, and then, in the dead of night, the sheikh despatched them, on fast donkeys, to the coast. Nor was this the only instance of Arab magnanimity, since during the Bushiri troubles, Rumaliza, the chief of Ujiji, saved the missionary, Mr. Swann, and his wife from the mob, and secretly despatched them, in a boat, down Tanganyika. As for Seef-bin-Saad, that excellent individual promptly accepted German pay, and was nominated Wali, or Governor of Tabora.

At best, these two men occupied, on our arrival, a singularly thankless post. The Wali was regarded as a renegade by the more fanatical Arabs, and welt in daily danger of his life. Herr von Siegl's position looked gloomy enough from the military point of view, while his civil administration partook, more or less, of the farcical. Some of the less powerful Arabs had, it is true, thought fit to depart, and carry on their nefarious commerce from Kasongo, and Nyangwé on the Congo. But the more crafty remained; and, while pursuing at home the peaceful occupations of agriculture and legitimate trade, sent their agents, well equipped with arms and ammunition, to raid the unresisting villages on the west of Tanganyika. The truth is, that the commandants of up-country stations do not receive fair play, either from the Congo Free State, or their own fellow-countrymen at Bagamoyo. On the river, the Belgians have no scruples about exchanging gunpowder for ivory; nor has Tippoo Tib discontinued his former malpractices despite his official wage of £1 per day as Governor of Stanley Falls. Indeed, while staying at Tabora, he told Herr von Siegl that all efforts to stop his enterprises would recoil upon their authors. "You Germans," said he, "may possibly hamper me in one direction, and the Belgian Anti-Slavery Society in another. But I can easily raise an army of a hundred and eighty thousand men in the Manyuema country. With these I shall march northwards, and find an outlet for my wares in the Soudan, where the Khalifa is already my co-religionist, and would gladly become my friend. If I undertake that ad-venture, those who oppose me shall speedily discover their mistake."

No doubt this utterance smacked strongly of gasconade. But, equally certain is it that, in spite of treaties and congresses, the Arabs' supply of ammunition is practically unlimited. We were actually told that Tippoo Tib's lieutenants, on the Upper Congo, drew a stock of fifty thousand pounds of powder annually from Bagamoyo. The statement must have been grossly exaggerated; but I was a personal witness to the fact that one of the caravans travelling with us, carried two hundred rifles and ten barrels of gunpowder, destined for the Manyuema country. Yet, immediately behind them marched Captain Jacques, on a mission for the suppression of slavery, which might necessitate a close acquaintance with those very weapons of war. If the nigger entertains a latent sense of humour, he must be vastly tickled by these strangely contradictory products of our much-vaunted civilization. And if officials, for the sake of revenue, persist in winking at these wholly illegal importations, how can the Powers escape, not only the charges of cant and avarice, but—what is far more calculated to produce amendment—some crushing military disaster?

Our stay at Tabora passed pleasantly enough. The Arabs were extremely courteous, and sent us numerous presents of fruit, vegetables, and bread, the last of which we had not tasted since leaving the French mission at Mrogro. That these attentions were entirely disinterested, we by no means ventured to flatter ourselves. The obvious explanation of their conduct lay in the fact that they hoped to profit by the presence of so many Europeans in Tabora to play off one party against the other. They had heard that Captain Jacques intended to operate against the slave-trade; and their attitude towards Captain von Siegl was, of course, that of perpetual hostility. Accordingly they overwhelmed the Englishmen with compliments, much as they would have caressed the German and scowled at the Briton, if we had been passing through the British East Africa Company's sphere. We naturally did not lend ourselves to their intrigues; but made use of their temporary good-will to gain promises of a clear road to Karema, and a supply of dhows for crossing the lake.

I visited several of these grandees, who were suffering from various ailments, at their houses; and I am bound to say that, whatever their morals may be, their manners would bear favourable comparison with those of any European aristocracy. One in particular, Ali-bin-Suleiman, overwhelmed me with gratitude and offers of presents, which somehow never reached their destination. However, the Arab, though his subsequent discretion outran the first impulses of generosity, was a very agreeable person, and conversed freely on the general situation. He complained most bitterly of German exactions, saying that they took provisions without payment, and treated the Mohammedans worse than dogs. After listening to a long tirade on this well-worn topic, I induced him to show me his establishment, built on the pattern that I have already described; and during the peregrination I was somewhat taken aback by the suggestion that one of his five wives should enter my harem. After stammering out some clumsy excuse for declining so unexpected a gift, I hastily took my leave. Ali-bin-Suleiman certainly present d a striking figure as we parted at the gateway. He was probably three parts negro, but his features were stamped with the distinction and intelligence of the superior race. Besides, his attire was most picturesque, consisting for headgear of a white burnous, while from his shoulders hung a dark robe, fringed with gold-lace, and thrown open in front to display a spotlessly clean cambric shirt.

The sheikh's charges against the Germans were, of course, exaggerated; nevertheless, the two races seemed hopelessly uncongenial. We were present, on several occasions, at the *baraza*, or council, at which the commercial and judicial affairs of Tabora were discussed between the Commandant and the leading Arabs. At this palaver the most delicate topics constantly emerged, nor were the offences alleged entirely confined to the latter community. Sometimes, for instance, a slave would rob his master, and then claim German protection. At another, Herr von Siegl's Soudanese soldiers would be convicted of straying into the *soko*, or marketplace, and appropriating sundry eatables. Here were matters evidently requiring tact and discretion, so that justice might be exercised by the administration, without unnecessary concessions, which would certainly be misconstrued. But at more than one sitting Teutonic militarism aggravated the original quarrel considerably, and the Wali's dignity was terribly ruffled; as when Herr von Siegl, for instance, in pure inadvertence, snatched a letter from his hand. The Arab, as a rule, is an adept at concealing his emotions; still, the look of cunning hatred which came over that man's face enabled the bystanders to read his mind as a book.

We had little to do with the Wali, but his donkey was one of the sights of Tabora. The "moke" might certainly claim to be queen of her race; for she stood fully fourteen hands, and, being of Muscat breed, was pure white. Until you looked at the ears, the general appearance was that of a fine Welsh cob. The proud owner valued her at two hundred dollars; and, though the price sounds a trifle stiff, the animal would create a perfect furore in the Park.

Hospitable though the Arabs were, we naturally found the society of Europeans more congenial. We had several dinners with Captain Jacques and his officers, for one of which the Marquis de

Bonchamps performed prodigies in the art of cookery. Here is the *menu*: ox-tail soup; *entrée*, stewed kidneys; joint, beefsteak; sweets, *compôte* of cakes, bananas, jam and rice; dessert, with bread and honey; tea and coffee, followed by whisky. Herr von Siegl also gave a dinner in our honour and, after apologizing for the absence of wine on the ground that he had received no stores from the coast since April, insisted on our drinking a bottle of hollands which had been presented to him the day before by Captain Jacques. Such extraordinary generosity naturally captivated us at once; and, apart from being a most agreeable man and a pointed conversationalist, he appeared thoroughly up to his work, and more than a match for the sharpest Arab on the station. His only helmet was perforated by a large bullet-hole received in one of his engagements with the Wangoni. We had several conversations with him about German East Africa, and found him most sanguine as to its prospects. At the same time his actual situation received a pertinent illustration from the fact that he was sending off the mail in charge of twenty askari, with orders that, if Makangi repeated his former tactics and turned it back, they were to cut their way through at all hazards. His chief topic was the burning one of missionaries, upon which he expressed himself in terms the reverse of complimentary. According to him, they are more occupied in building fine houses for their families than in attending to their flocks, and he had a very poor opinion of the native convert. This person he declared to be a rogue at the outset; to behave fairly well while immediately under his pastor's eye; but added that, directly he returned to his native village, savage instincts immediately reasserted themselves, while the knowledge acquired at the mission station was used to establish a tyranny over the stay-at-home nigger. From this sweeping censure he expressly excluded Mr. Price, of Mpwapwa, and Mr. Hooper of Mombasa, both of whom he allowed to be thoroughly pious and conscientious men. I am bound to say that, from what we saw of the missionaries at Blantyre and elsewhere I can by no means endorse this wholesale condemnation.

After dinner the commandant treated us to a grand spectacle in a war-dance of his Wangoni soldiers. These fine fellows had only entered his service three weeks previously, when the chief of the tribe sent his son with twenty-five warriors, saying that they should form the body-guard of the Great White Leader. Well; they marched in the barrack-yard bearing on their heads busbies like those of our

Foot Guards, but made of feathers instead of bearskin. Their arms consisted of three heavy spears and a shield of buffalo hide, and their uniform, a loin-cloth excepted, was that provided by nature. The chief's son was distinguished by a brown leather tail to his headgear, the others wearing a black tag. At first they advanced four deep, singing the while in a low monotone which gradually swelled into a full-volumed cry. Having arrived at the position, they halted two deep with admirable exactness; when the chief's son began the dance. This ceremony consisted in bounding thrice along the line, while the performer chanted some song of victory. Each of his twenty-five soldiers performed the same evolution, and then the whole band advanced to the audience, and, falling on the knees, exclaimed in a simultaneous shout, "You are all right noble men." The whole performance was attended by a consciousness of savage courage and chivalry, which an artist might reproduce, but which can hardly be conveyed in words.

The bearing of these uncivilized barbarians appeared the more striking, when contrasted with a like performance on the part of our Zanzibaris, witnessed by the Marquis de Bonchamps and myself, while strolling next evening round the town. They formed two groups, one of the Mombasa men, and the other of the Zanzibaris proper, or rather improper. The former contented themselves with crossing the circle and returning to an accompaniment of hand-clapping, varied by a doggerel refrain The latter heroes had provided their show with the additional attractions of some Wanyamwesi women, and several drums. The din of these instruments was augmented by prodigious yells; while the whole circle wheeled round from left to right, each performer being apparently free to assert his individuality by the wildest gestures. It is perhaps unnecessary to say that, though the invention was elaborate, it tended to suggestions of indecency. Our men, by the way, had become great bucks in these days, and shone with the oil of gladness. Also they no longer went barefoot, as on the march, but stalked about in sandals, which, like the Arabs, they slipped off before entering a house. It was a great sight to see a Zanzibari party "doing the heavy" through Tabora.

One morning, as I was coming from the Wali's, a large group of natives caught my attention. They stood closely packed together, and listened as though entranced to a blind Wanyamwesi singer. The man had a beautiful tenor voice; and his stirring airs differed altogether from the droning monotone which the nigger vocalist, as a rule, affects. Moreover the language lends itself to music, as its vowel sounds resemble the Italian not a little. In fact, the whole performance gave distinct pleasure, and would not have disgraced a London concert hall At his third song the people seemed strangely moved, and I was informed by an onlooker that the ballad celebrated the glories of Mirambo the Deliverer. Evidently the sentiment of patriotism has been by no means extinguished in this intellectual race by its present misfortunes.

Captain Stairs was very busy during these days in hiring porters to replace those we had engaged at Mamboya. The rest of us were occupied in reducing the loads, by selecting such baggage as would least encumber our march to Karema. The remainder was left in charge of Herr von Siegl, who kindly undertook to store it in case we returned that way. On the 20th, Captain Stairs had finished his preparations, aid decided to start for Karema the following morning. As I had several patients, including a Wangoni soldier and two officers of Captain Jacques', it was decided that I should remain at Tabora for a day, and rejoin the caravan by a series of forced marches. The road being reported dangerous, I applied for a competent *Nyampara*, and, greatly to my satisfaction, secured Hamadi, by far the steadiest and most capable of the lot. Accordingly, at 9.30 a.m., the expedition wound out of Tabora, after I had received a most effusive farewell from the porters, who shook me by the hand, and hoped they would soon see me again. This affection, we may suspect, was inspired by lively hope of favours to come.

The Wangoni was suffering from a bullet in the leg, received during the war with Captain von Siegl. The latter asked me to extract it; but he appeared much surprised when I arrived to perform operation, declaring that no doctor, within knowledge, ever made good a promise. Evidently the youth was a sceptic in other matters besides proselytism. The man was held down by a Soudanese sergeant; and though the pain must have been extreme, he did not utter a single shout, and merely groaned twice or thrice. Any European would have been completely prostrated by the shock and fever; but this singularly constituted savage was discovered that evening seated with the most perfect unconcern before a large chunk of goat's flesh.

Captain Jacques' two officers were down with fever, and one of them, M. Vrithoff, had a very severe attack. Though medical details may possibly prove caviare to the majority of readers, yet the case is sufficiently curious to warrant a brief account. When I first saw M. Vrithoff his temperature stood very high, at 102° in the morning and 104° in the evening. Quinine was administered in three doses of ten grains apiece; and I left him that night with strict orders to take very little solid nourishment, merely chicken broth and bread and milk. Next day I called at 10.30 a.m., and found my patient walking about and intent upon his daily routine. A lecture upon the folly of not being in bed was stopped by Captain Jacques; who told me that M. Vrithoff had eaten six eggs and a large helping of meat, and that the fever had completely disappeared. I was so completely taken aback, that I went off without saying a word. On the morrow, while attending the other officer, I heard that the foolhardiness of the day before had been punished by a return of sickness; and sure enough M. Vrithoff's temperature stood at 103° about midday, and rose to 104.6° in the evening. An injection was administered; and at 5.45 next morning his temperature had dropped to 101.4°, and had become normal by 8 p.m. Next day the improvement continued; so I was able to prescribe a light diet, with quinine, iron, and arsenic, without much fear of a dangerous relapse.

Captain Stairs' instructions were that I should not stay at Tabora a day longer than was absolutely necessary; and of course the longer the delay, the greater would be the leeway to be made up. Accordingly, on the morning of the 14th, I told Captain Jacques that my orders compelled me to "hump my swag," and he entirely concurred. We parted, therefore, with hopes of meeting again at Karema; and at 6.30 a.m. my little caravan marched out of Tabora.

Chapter VI

Ugunda and Ugalla

A forced march—A troop of baboons—Seke—An interview with Munchara—Joma's slumbers—A ticklish march—Ugunda—Bark cloth—Native uncleanliness—A dancing man—My cook deserts—Fever again—Captain Stairs' sickness—Zanzibari inhumanity—Death of Bull—Beasts and birds—White ants— A hippo hunt—A feast of fat things—Mashodi and the lion— A bellicose boar—A bushfire—The Ugalla country—A ruga-ruga—The Wagalla—Gongwé and its heads—An inefficient Watch—Native artisans—The Marquis' wroth—Mouhari—Slave Caravans—We ascend the mountains—Tanganyika at last.

THE small band, that was hastening to catch up Captain Stairs, consisted of one nyampara (Hamadi), an askari, twelve porters, three boys, one cook, and myself. The men had become very soft after their three weeks' idleness, and began to "cry a go" before they had been many hours on the road. The soldier Juma had also been drinking heavily before leaving Tabora, and seemed in a hopelessly lethargic and befuddled condition. Accordingly we made a short stage, and halted at 9.30 a.m.; otherwise there would have been several invalids on the march to Karema. The camp was called Mruma, and had been occupied by Captain Stairs during the previous night. Late in the afternoon he sent a message that he was encamped at Mtoni, six miles further west; and intended to halt there for the following day.

We had hardly pitched the tents, when the most unearthly noise was heard away to the right. For the moment there were apprehensions of attack; but the clamour proved to be caused by a troop of baboons, in full cry after some village dogs, the former chattering and the latter yelping with fear. I went to the assistance of the friends of man, and effected a diversion by wounding one of the apes. The herd thereupon took refuge upon some neighbouring rocks; and, the females with their young having been despatched to a safe elevation, the males stood their ground with amazingly human gestures of anger and defiance. A second shot would doubtless have created a stampede, but they were permitted to claim a moral victory. These beasts travel the country in gangs some hundreds strong, with sentinels and chiefs of companies. Their descents upon the crops are much dreaded by the natives, whose indifferent weapons cannot cope with the agile brigands. Indeed, cultivated fields have sometimes to be abandoned in consequence of their persistent depredations. The monkeys tried the men's nerves the more, because we were halting in very dangerous country. The king of the district, Seke by name, boasted a lineage of unknown antiquity, and was titular sovereign of Unyanyembe. Unable, however, to hold his own against the Arabs, and defeated in more than one engagement by Herr von Siegl, he had been compelled to put up with the status of sub-chieftain. Possibly the loss of dignity had soured his temper; at any rate, Seke was notoriously hostile to strangers, and had little scruples about cutting up a weak caravan. A practical proof of his disposition had been given us, before we left Tabora, by the murder of one of our porters. The unfortunate fellow, who was a Wanyamwesi, had been allowed by Captain Stairs to visit his relations; and on his way back Seke's retainers fell upon him, and performed the unhappy despatch. Redress was promptly demanded and as readily promised; but the will, according to barbarian ethics, had to be taken for the deed. The strength of the Stairs expedition would naturally cause him to be chary of attack; still the temptation to surround our weak detachment must have been considerable, more especially as his malignity found strengthening arguments in his greed for cloth and ammunition.

  In the afternoon one of his dependents appeared in Camp, and informed me that his name was Munchara, and that he was headman of the neighbouring village. Munchara did not take after his master; for he beamed hospitality, and actually brought as a present a goat and a quantity of flour. In return I gave him a red silk handkerchief with which he seemed vastly pleased, and then, in a spirit of weak amiability, I promised to treat any sick persons in his *tembé*. After an hour's absence, he returned with some thirty niggers at his heels, who were suffering from every form of malady, from leprosy to a chafed toe. This liberal interpretation of my pledge naturally threatened to empty the medicine-chest; however, I doctored the worst cases and persuaded the others that imagination played a great part in their illnesses. After the medical *séance* they all sat round the tent, and began to examine my possessions with the curiosity common to the Wanyamwesi race. Some of my most precious garments seemed in danger of evaporating into space as they passed from hand to hand; when I luckily recollected that one of my old books of medicine contained a coach-builder's advertisement, representing glorified landaus and spirited, if impossible, steeds. The volume was produced, and caused the most unbounded satisfaction. The horses were greeted at once with delighted cries of "Donkey! donkey!"; and one talented son of Ham remarked that the white men cut off their animals' ears. The carriages, however, posed the assemblage considerably; some maintaining them to be a species of centipede, others a great medicine or idol. After an attempted explanation, the drift of which concerned a canoe moving on dry land, I was forced to give up the exposition of the unknown. Munchara—who smelt abominably by the way—professed to have derived the most solid instruction from the lecture; and the party went away in the highest of spirits.

The night passed anxiously enough; as, despite Munchara's natural amiability, his overlord might have given orders for a night attack, with the alternative of decapitation. Accordingly I had the loads placed within my tent, and went the sounds at intervals of an hour or so. On each occasion Juma was discovered sleeping the sleep of the toper, and he appeared absolutely insensible to threats or blows. I was glad enough when morning dawned, and we could resume our stern chase.

Arrived at Mtoni at 9 p.m., we discovered that the caravan had marched some six miles further. This information was conveyed by a note which Captain Stairs had placed on a high bush, and the missive went on to say that we had best be on our guard against the natives. The warning was repeated on various pieces of paper which he had posted upon trees along the road. We descended some enchanting glades, resembling the scenery of a well- wooded English park; and then passed within three hundred yards of the redoubtable Seke's own village. Fortunately no hostile demonstration was made, but still the situation was none too reassuring. Hamadi led the way, prepared to shoot down any amount of assailants, and I brought up the rear. Our two selves excepted, we knew that the appearance of a score of spearmen would be immediately followed by a general stampede;

though Seydik, the tent porter. swore, as Bob Acres, by his valour. Then we missed the track; and did not hit it again, until half an hour had been cut to waste. Just before noon my eyes were gladdened by the sight of the familiar tent-tops, and we received a most enthusiastic reception. The whole camp turned out in our honour; and while some of the pagazi relieved my men of their loads, others rushed to grasp me by the hand. The most delicate attention was that paid me by the chief Amani, who, coming up, took my rifle from me, after I had carried it for six hours under a broiling sun. Having presented my report to Captain Stairs, I thankfully accepted Bodson's invitation to lunch, and kept quiet for the remainder of the day.

The country of Ugunda, through which we were now passing, is fairly level and suitable for cultivation. The water is reasonably good, and the abundance of timber proves that it must be stored close to the surface. Some of the trees are distinctly imposing, particularly a species of fig, from the bark of which the natives manufacture cloth. This is done by stripping off the outer rind, and swathing the inner layer with leaves and grass. When it has become quite soft, it is taken off, steeped in water, and then beaten with little hammers until a material is produced resembling a rough drugget. Some of the smaller trees were covered with leaves, though the dry season had nearly elapsed.

The bark-cloth industry obtains also among the Wanyamwesi; nor do the natives of Ugunda differ greatly from that tribe either in appearance or language. The attire, however, is considerably scantier; the men wearing merely a loin-cloth, and the women contenting themselves with a very limited apron. Their repute is none of the best, since they are reported to be treacherous and predatory. We met, however, with no molestation; as they appeared bent upon getting the ground ready for the *masika*, or rainy season. The villages are large, and surrounded by fields of *matamah* and sweet potatoes, varied by groves of bananas. Distance, however, decidedly lent enchantment; as on approaching them the nostrils were assailed by the most overpowering stench, resulting from the complete neglect of sanitary precautions. As several of these *tembés* were, in addition, built close to stagnant water, we were at a loss to imagine why the whole population did not succumb to fever and ague.

The Wagunda are keen traders, and frequently came into camp with articles for sale. One enterprising dealer produced an English-made padlock, which had travelled, somehow, from the coast; though, as the key had been lost, it hardly appeared a negotiable article of commerce. Our most popular visitor, however, was a dancing man, who went through his performance one afternoon, to the intense delight of the porters. The exhibition was a trifle suggestive, but at the same time by no means devoid of grace. In particular the movements of the body were so elaborate, that we could only conclude the vertebrae to be made of indiarubber. For accompaniment, he tapped a small drum with one finger; and concluded with whirling contortions of arms and legs, notably the well-known "twist", which would have evoked the wildest demonstrations of approval from the gallery of a London music- hall. The Zanzibaris, for that matter, were by no means a cold audience.

Two days afterwards, a chief—the obsequious Amani—deserted, together with a pagazi and my cook. The plot, so far as the last was concerned, had been brewing for some time; indeed, rumours to that effect had reached my ears before we attained Tabora. Throughout the expedition he had behaved with sulky superiority, seldom condescending to prepare a respectable meal, though his capacities were reasonably proficient. Thence unpleasantness ensued; and when I heard at Tabora that the skulker had been seen in confabulation with an Arab hailing from Ujiji, I daily expected that he would give me the slip. The fellow probably perceived that my suspicions were aroused, and therefore waited for a more favourable opportunity before betaking himself to his new master. At any rate, the runaways' strategy was completely successful, as we never discovered the slightest trace of their movements. Captain Stairs kindly provided me with a substitute for the fugitive chef; but, though willing enough, he proved extremely incompetent; and I was glad to secure the assistance of Charles, a porter who had been taught the elements of cleanliness at the Mombasa mission.

Fever is endemic among the Wagunda, and that of malignant kind, haematuria being one of its concomitant symptoms. Several of the porters were soon down with the disease; and Saleh, one of Captain Bodson's boys, was for several days dangerously ill, the visitation being the more severe because he was copper-coloured arid not black. The first of the Europeans to succumb was the unfortunate Robinson, who had been attacked before we landed at Bagamoyo, and suffered more or less the whole way to Tabora. His discomfort was increased by the loss of his donkey, which died in Tigogo; nevertheless, he stuck most gallantly to his work, and gradually picked up strength. On the night of the 25th he had a serious relapse, with vertigo and general weakness; but from that time his health improved, and on reaching Karema he was fairly himself again.

Even more alarming was the illness of Captain Stairs, which began on the 19th of September, and continued until the end of the month. He had a dangerous attack of haematuric fever; nor did his persistent refusal to acknowledge that anything was amiss, tend to allay my anxieties. At the most he consented to ride on ahead of the *safari* in the early morning, in order to reach the camp before the sun became powerful. On the 24th we all implored him to suspend the march for a day. or two, so as to give himself a chance of recovery; but the only answer to be obtained was, "I have undertaken to reach Karema on the 9th of October, and on that day I intend to be there." Next day his debility was extreme, and he had to be carried in a hammock by four men. This condition of comparative inactivity became unendurable to him on the 26th; and he informed me that he intended to leave the hammock after the morrow at all risks, and march with the caravan, as people "played about" in his absence. Certain it was that, directly his watchful eye was removed, everybody began to take matters easily; and the start, which should have been at six o'clock, was frequently delayed until 6.30. According to his determination, he mounted his donkey on the 28th, and gradually began to mend. At the same time, I could see that his constitution was far less robust than he imagined, and that prolonged exertion would probably result in a breakdown. Unfortunately he was generally at high pressure, keenly ambitious of the expedition's success, and unable, therefore, to rest satisfied, unless acquainted with the smallest detail. If the hackneyed expression, "a martyr to duty", can be applied to any man, it can be used without fear of contradiction of Captain Stairs.

It was not long before I had some thirty-five men on the sick list with various kinds of fever; nor did the experiment of camping in the native villages prove an entire success, as the advantage gained by the better shelter from the sun was neutralized by the foetid atmosphere. There was little or no wind, and the atmospheric thermometer sometimes registered 132°. The nights, also, were terribly oppressive; and it was while going the rounds at a late hour, that I came across a terrible instance of Zanzibari inhumanity. Among the porters were a father and son, and the man's wife had also chosen to accompany the expedition. The wretched boy was attacked by fever, and while in that condition was absolutely neglected by his parents, who left him without food for three days. The result was a complete collapse, and he expired next morning soon after the march had begun. I naturally remained behind until life was extinct; but not so the stony-hearted authors of his being, who left camp, without even looking into the hut, to bid their son a last farewell. The story may appear almost incredible; but equally glaring instances of the nigger's indifference to the family tie occurred after the expedition reached Katanga.

Another death, which happened about this stage of the journey, was that of Captain Bodson's Congo dog (a sort of lurcher) Bull. The poor beast was brought into camp one evening, covered with wounds and greatly exhausted by loss of blood. His owner imagined that a buffalo was to blame, but the teeth-marks of some large baboon were plainly visible. I doctored Bull to the best of my ability; but he never rallied, and died in the night. He was a great favourite with the porters, who displayed considerably more grief for his loss than one of their confraternity would probably have evoked.

Man might be vile in Ugunda, but the prospect pleased, the succession of woods and dales being most captivating to the eye. Big game abounded; but it was extremely difficult to get a shot, as the herds of antelope and zebras seldom approached within six miles of the caravan. When Captain Stairs rode ahead of the line, he used to see several hundred head in one march; but the beasts speedily winded the *safari*, and disappeared. The Marquis de Bonchamps went out in quest of game every afternoon, with praiseworthy pertinacity; and at last succeeded in bagging an antelope and three wild pigs. The last proved, by the way, rather a superfluity, as the porters, being Mohammedans, would not touch the meat. These porkers travel in large droves, and are very destructive. Indeed we passed a village-site which had been abandoned, partly because of a quarrel with a neighbouring settlement, but chiefly on account of the swine's depredations upon the crops. The inhabitants had accordingly left the place, and were engaged in building a new *tembé*, a march nearer Tanganyika. Birds were equally numerous: we saw vultures for the first time since we had left Usagara; swallows flitted round the native huts; and water-wagtails, closely resembling the English species, ran about within a yard of a person keeping fairly still. The ornithologist, however, would have been most captivated by a dark green bird, the size of a thrush, which flew from tree to tree, in numerous flocks. Its plumage was simply perfect, and shone in the sunlight like burnished metal.

These fowls of the air had meat in abundance, since the whole country swarmed with white ants. After rain they covered the ground, and the wagtails crammed their crops at pleasure; again, the insects in their winged stage fell easy victims to those industrious little hunters. In both Ugunda and Ugalla, as in other parts of the Central African plateau, the ant-heaps form a distinctive feature in the landscape. They are sometimes from fifteen to twenty feet high; and their age can be guessed from the full-grown trees which emerge from the pyramid-shaped structures, containing tons of earth. Moreover, you frequently pass through whole forests in which the trunks are covered with the earthen tunnels built by the insects, in order to attain some decayed branch, upon which they feed in security from their would-be persecutors. King Solomon's sluggard could hardly fail to be suddenly converted, if he visited those subtropical highlands.

At last, near one of Commander Cameron's old camps, we obtained some real good sport. It was situated close to a river, which flowed at the bottom of a rocky valley, overhung by the virgin forest. Owing to the prolonged drought, the stream had contracted into a series of deep pools, in one of which some twenty hippos were disporting themselves. A porter, who had gone down for water, promptly gave the signal; and within a few minutes Bonchamps, Bodson, and myself were seated on the banks, and waiting for one of the huge beasts to come up to breathe. The instant a nostril appeared, crack went the rifles; and a faint red streak was visible on the water, as the animals sank again with a gurgle. Whether it was that the yelling of an enthusiastic ring of Zanzibaris unsteadied our aim, or that these particular hippos possessed abnormally thick hides, at any rate they took a deal of killing. After about four hours of somewhat wild firing, four huge carcases were floating on the water with grey upturned bellies; the remainder broke away, under cover of a bed of rushes, and could be heard crashing down the river-bed. The next difficulty was how to get our game to shore. The porters declined to wade, shouting "Crocodile, crocodile!", and there was every probability that they had deviated into truth. At length some one suggested the device of a heavy bough, tied to a rope, and then dragged down the pool. After several failures, resulting in the prostration of pagazi by the score, the primitive tackle held; and with much shouting and splashing the hippos were hauled on land.

When food is plentiful, Zanzibaris decline to eat hippo, on account of the beast's resemblance to the pig forbidden by the Prophet. Those scruples, however, disappeared before the compelling power of a week's short commons, and the camp was speedily converted into a redolent slaughter-house. In a twinkling the beasts had been hacked to pieces, and huge steaks were broiling before the fires. As the process of cooking appeared tantalizingly slow, each man was armed in addition with a wooden skewer, upon which he toasted nine or ten titbits. These speedily vanished with the action of a boy swallowing a lollipop, and then the slab of meat was attacked while still practically raw. Upon this the fellows gorged themselves until they could gorge no more; then they went off to sleep, with the unfinished portion close at hand. Several times during the night they awoke, had another "tuck in", and dropped again into stertorous slumber. It is needless to say that on the following day the start was effected with anything but celerity, and that the *doctari* was pestered with complaints of stomach- ache. Luckily for the gluttons, the march was a short one, and by the morrow the elastic Zanzibari systems had thrown off the effects of repletion. I should say that the European officers were by no means contemptuous of hippo-steak, which tastes like a very reasonably toothsome blend of beef and pork.

The hippo-hunt, by the way, was not the only excitement of this eventful day, since, just before sundown, a porter rushed into camp with the news that the chief Massoudi was "treed" by a lion. We seized our rifles and sallied forth, to discover the nyampara perched on a lofty fork, and uttering incoherent ejaculations in Swahili. The perspiration streamed down his intelligent countenance, which had perceptibly turned a shade or two lighter than the ordinary. Indeed, we afterwards learnt that he had almost stumbled on the beast; and, but for a warning growl, would have been *non est* before we could possibly have come to the rescue. Unfortunately our efforts to get a shot at his assailant proved entirely futile. When we arrived he had retired into the jungle, and declined to stir for any amount of beating and yelling. Less lucky than a certain noble sportsman in Mashonaland, we never succeeded in bagging a lion during the whole expedition.

A still more ludicrous incident occurred a few days afterwards, when a very large wild boar charged the caravan. Some fifty porters threw down their loads *instanter*; some making for the trees, and others rushing headlong into the bush. A more complete panic it would be impossible to imagine; and I remember being struck with the adroitness with which Robinson snatched his rifle from one of the boys, who would otherwise have hurled it to perdition in hi terror. The brute came down the path like a thunderbolt; and though one of the chiefs fired point-blank, it did not appear to be hit, and, before the absurdity of the situation had been fully realized, was out of sight. The affair, of course, could only be viewed as a comedy; still it left behind it certain disquieting reflections as to the possible upshot of an attack by a more formidable foe.

On the 27th of September we were menaced by a very serious disaster, as some careless pagazi contrived to set the bush on fire during the march. The starting-point of the flames lay off the road, but they made incredible headway, and the porters strove in vain to keep under the conflagration. Fortunately, the wind drove it to the south-west; otherwise the rear-guard would have been overwhelmed, and another chapter added to the history of African disaster. As usual, the culprit could not be discovered; since the more thickly evidence accumulated upon any individual, the more elaborate and convincing were his disclaimers.

The Ugalla country, through which we were now travelling, is covered with jungle (*pori*), varied by the primeval forest. The scenery in the latter was most imposing; tree was bound to tree by festoons of sweet-smelling creepers, while here and there some giant of the woods towered above his brethren. The greenery and the shade made the march comparatively tolerable, in spite of the heavens being as a furnace above. Also we were able to stalk big game in the long grass with considerable success. The Marquis shot two zebras in one afternoon, and so the porters were provided with meat in abundance. In other respects this stage of the journey was rather laborious, since the quantity of fallen timber rendered the carriage of the boat sections terribly arduous. Further, several porters were unable to resist the temptation of the winding paths, and deserted. One malingerer, however, was discovered by two nyamparas in a village, and brought to a sense of duty by a sound flogging.

One morning I was suddenly confronted on the road by a *ruga-ruga*, or robber. He was a fine specimen of humanity, and had evidently spent some care over his personal adornment. From his shoulders hung a leopard's skin; his long hair was twisted in rope-like masses; and large bracelets of beads decorated his neck, wrists, and ankles. For weapons he carried a bow and arrows, a small hatchet, and a small dagger-shaped knife worn in a sheath on the left arm. I beckoned him to approach; but he appeared extremely suspicious of our intentions, and it was only when I laid down my rifle that he consented to stand. Even when I came up he kept edging away, and had to be forcibly detained by a hand laid on his wrist. As he was ignorant of Swahili, one of the chiefs acted as interpreter, to whom the *ruga-ruga* volunteered the information that he was carrying a message to a chief in Ugunda. The statement seemed very dubious, as his actions were those of one on the prowl. I showed him a handkerchief, and his eyes glistened with desire. When, however, the chief offered it in exchange for the little dagger, the pride of ownership prevailed, and a long confabulation took place before the bargain was effected. Finally the interesting outlaw took his leave; and lost no time in placing a considerable distance between himself and the caravan, without once casting a backward glance.

The Wagalla, taken as a whole, are by no means blessed with a superabundance of energy. They clear just enough of the forest to satisfy their daily wants, and in the space thus created *matamah* and rice are cultivated in a very perfunctory fashion. They own no oxen, only a few goats, and a vast quantity of fowls. Hence eggs were abundant; and an askari of Captain Bodson's, Mahommed Moti, whose foraging abilities had become proverbial in the caravan, used to buy up the stock in every village, and retail it at exorbitant prices. The *tembés* are large and surrounded by the usual palisade, which, thanks to the dampness of the soil, frequently takes root and becomes a living rampart. The natives differ widely in appearance from those of Unyanyembe and Ugunda. These last generally shave the crown of the head, and plait the hair with fibres of bark-cloth, so that it lies close to the skull. The Wagalla, on the contrary, allow their locks to grow, and then twist them into horns arid tufts similar to those affected by the Wagogo. They also resemble that race in wearing a quantity of heavy anklets, and bracelets of brass and copper. One dandy was bedecked with a necklace of empty revolver-cartridges, and this peculiarity of adornment evidently caused him no little satisfaction. As for the women they follow no particular fashion in dressing the hair or in costume. The usual scanty petticoat suffices, and the superior sex monopolizes the family jewellery.

On the 2nd of October we encamped in the village of Gongwé, lying about three miles to the south of a very lofty mountain of the same name, with another range about seven miles away on the opposite side. We found the inhabitants busily engaged in rebuilding the huts, half of which had been burnt down. On inquiring the cause of the disaster we learnt that the people of Ugunda had attacked the place on two successive nights, shortly before our arrival. On each occasion they were beaten off with considerable loss; but on the second they succeeded in firing the boma, and at one moment the village was in danger of being totally consumed. The chief, who seemed a decidedly capable man, managed to exercise his authority with such effect, that part of his forces went in pursuit of the enemy, while the remainder suppressed the flames. The former business must have been effected with workmanlike conscientiousness, since sixteen Wagunda were taken captive. In keeping with the amenities of native warfare, their heads, stuck on poles, grinned at the traveller, in uncanny fashion, as he approached the west gate of the village. It was a curious sight to see the children playing under these ghastly trophies with entire absence of concern, though they would have scared a European baby into convulsions. The victorious Wagalla, on the other hand, had by no means got off unscathed, and some of those wounded in the action came to me for advice. One man had been hit in the chest; and, as the bone was diseased, I persuaded him to consent to its removal. Unluckily the chief's permission had to be obtained as well; and that worthy absolutely declined to countenance the operation, saying that no medicine man could perform so great a miracle. Owing to this perverse scepticism on the part of a paternal government, the unlucky hero had to be left to his fate.

As we were encamped among such a warlike people, it was necessary to see that our sentries were on the alert. However, on turning out early in the morning to look after the boats, I discovered the askari in charge fast asleep. Curiously enough, I had left him the night before in the last extremity of terror, thinking that every moment would be his last. He was somewhat reassured on discovering that other soldiers stood on duty by the loads, and his false alarms must have given place to an equally fictitious security. Fortunately for the expedition, the Wagalla appeared to have given over all thoughts of fighting, and to be intent on the arts of peace. They wore busily engaged in planting their fields; while the rain-god was piously invoked by little models of huts like those we had seen in Unyanyembe, and tiny platforms, intended apparently to serve as bedsteads, when it pleased him to rest.

The Wagalla are a very neat-handed race, and manufacture cloth from cotton as well as bark. I watched two men at work one morning; and, considering the primitive character of their machines, they turned out an exceedingly finished material. The younger partner was making yarn; and the first process consisted in working the cotton, with the finger and thumb, into a fiat tape, about two yards long. This was hooked to a spindle, about a foot in length, which was rolled along the thigh so as to acquire a swift twirling motion; while the artist used his right forefinger and thumb, to prevent the thread from becoming unduly thick. When a length of yarn was spun, he handed it to the older man; who wound it upon shuttles about four feet long, and, plying them with the deftness of an old lady at her knitting, produced a cloth which, though exceedingly coarse in texture, seemed strong and very fairly regular. Unlike the ordinary nigger, the pair stuck to their task with praiseworthy industry, and appeared to experience a genuine pleasure from the handicraft. The pottery, also, at Gongwé, was decidedly superior to that in use among the Wagunda; and had evidently been made by one endowed with a sense of symmetry, some of the spiral ornamentation being decidedly effective.

After leaving Gongwé, a series of misadventures tried our various tempers somewhat severely. Thus, one night, a lion roared for hours round the camp, preventing any one from getting a wink of sleep. Next afternoon, my donkey walked into the Marquis de Bonchamps' tent, and entirely disorganized its usual neatness. My boy, Abdullah Mizé, was promptly castigated therefore; but the marquis had no one on whom to vent his wrath, when, just as we were pitching tents after a long day's march, Captain Stairs decided that the *safari* must proceed again, as the water was undrinkable. Whereupon Gallic indignation waxed uncontrollable—if this was Stanley's training, the less said of it the better; never had an expedition been arranged in such a careless manner; men ought to have been sent ahead, and so forth. However, Stanley or no Stanley, we had to tramp until 2.30 p.m., and then halted in a plain without an atom of shade. Owing to my cook's incompetency, I did not get my breakfast until 4.30 p.m. I remember well how that evening, while feeling utterly dejected and "down on my luck", I heard some of the porters, who had served on English vessels, begin to sing *The Bay of Biscay*, followed by *Home, Sweet Home* and *God save the Queen*. The flood of recollections evoked by those familiar ditties was so strong, that I could hardly bear to remain within their hearing.

On the 6th of October we halted outside a village called Kamba; and as the chief and his son, a child of ten years old, were down with fever, I went in to minister to their necessities. Mouhari, a stalwart gentleman, about thirty-five years of age, greeted me, according to the local custom, by clapping his hands six or seven times. According to strict etiquette, I should have returned the compliment, by slapping, in addition, first my left side and then my right; but the full ceremony was politely waived, in consideration of my being a stranger to the neighbourhood. Mouhari favoured me with a copious autobiography; of which the salient facts appeared to be that he had emigrated from Gongwé some three years previously, and was blessed with five and twenty wives. He seemed to place the greatest confidence in his medicine man, though the latter's remedies were not particularly recondite. He had tied a piece of rope round the chief's head, and plastered the boy's forehead with a reddish powder, made of antelope's teeth. Under the circumstances, one was hardly surprised to discover that fever was raging through the village.

We met several Arab caravans moving to and from Karema, some engaged in legitimate trade, but others in the slave traffic. The former were extremely courteous, and sent us some *kus-kus*, a national dish composed of rice and goat's-flesh. Their more nefarious fellow-countrymen seemed rather afraid of consequences, and kept out of our way. They were reported to be very numerous; and there was a huge caravan of seven hundred slaves travelling a few miles to the south, which had crossed the lake somewhere below Karema. One day we passed a small caravan, some twenty strong, composed of miserable creatures, who had been captured on the farther side of Tanganyika. They were tied together by ropes connected with wooden handcuffs, and appeared utterly dejected and exhausted by travel. Their brutal masters drove them along the road with plentiful applications of the stick, and the whole scene presented a squalid epitome of oppression and barbarism. The Arabs seemed to have lost their customary good manners in their degrading profession; since one Khalfan-Khalafeen, to whom I sent some medicine, apparently considered thanks superfluous.

The 8th of October found us within two marches of Karema and the porters, who had previously been morose, grew wild with excitement. Those with the boats were with difficulty kept in hand, as they seemed bent upon getting ahead of Captain Stairs. Hamadi, however, proved an excellent disciplinarian and restrained their exuberant energies. Nor was it long before he found an efficient ally in the difficulty of the road. We crossed a large river several times, and varied this proceeding by marching along the bed. It was ankle-deep in sand, and speedily caused some of the most capable to flag. Next day, after travelling for an hour and a half along the bank, we crossed some rice-fields, and reached the foot of the mountains separating us from Karema. Then we began to ascend a very steep pass, and attained the top utterly spent arid leg-weary. Still no Tanganyika; but, in obedience to Hamadi's advice, I proceeded with several of the chiefs to scale a small eminence to the left of the defile. We were rewarded by a most magnificent panorama. Behind us stretched the forests and plains of Ugalla; in front lay the lake with its azure waters dancing in the sunlight. The absolute stillness was broken only by a bird or two rising under our feet, and a film of cloud floating overhead. So entirely maritime was the prospect, that away to the north the heavens met the waters; and it was not until turning to the west that you perceived, on the farther side, the mighty shoulders of Mount Mrumbi. A moment's silence, and the men began to shout with joy. I raised a cheer, which was answered from below by Captain Stairs. Hamadi alone remained absolutely impassive, contenting himself with the remark, "Magi, bwana" ("Water, master"), uttered in a complacent tone. As an old hand at African travel, he evidently felt that his dignity would be compromised by any display of enthusiasm. Then we hurried down to rejoin our companions, and began the descent upon Karema.

CHAPTER VII

KAREMA

The first view of Karema—The French mission—The take's rise and fall—Its fauna—The native fishermen—Approach of the *masika*—The dhows—The steel boats—The passage begins— The mission's prospects—Arrival of Captain Jacques—Alarming symptoms in Captain Stairs—His views on German East Africa—Teutonic militarism—Ivory versus agriculture—Inadequacy of garrisons—The smuggling of arms and ammunition—The Arab.

THE caravan plunged down the mountain-side, through a narrow gully flanked by precipitous boulders. Suddenly, on rounding a spur of the lower slopes, we perceived Karema at our feet. The fort had been built nearly twelve years previously by Captain Cambier of that African International Association, whence has emerged the Congo Free State. Consequently, upon the redistribution of territory, it has since passed into German possession; and the French mission of White Fathers from Algeria, one of Cardinal Lavigerie's numerous efforts, has been allowed to take over the station. Karema is well placed from a military point of view; being situated on a small mound, which dominates the surrounding level. The defences consist of a wall, constructed nearly square, of sun-dried bricks without any moat, above which rises the roof of an inner house, surmounted by a primitive wooden cross. Round this place of refuge nestle the huts of the natives, the chapel, a carpenter's shop, and a large fowl-house. Away to the north stretch the mission's plantations of wheat, European potatoes, rice, beans, citrons, and bananas; mingled with the native fields of *matamah*, Indian corn, *mhoga* (manioc), and *viazi* (sweet potato). The prospect would be pleasant enough were it not for the complete absence of shade. The Fathers, unfortunately, have not succeeded in making trees grow on the plain; though the hills beyond are covered with palms, and the *mteva*, or fan-tree, which retains its leaves throughout the dry season.

As we approached the fort, a considerable multitude could be descried waiting to give us a welcome. It consisted of the Father Superior and five brothers, surrounded by a gesticulating posse of natives. The civilizing influence of the missionaries was at once perceptible in the conduct of the children, who crowded round the pagazi, whereas in the ordinary village they will run away at the approach of a stranger. After receiving a most kindly greeting and liberal offers of hospitality, we marched down to the beach and there encamped. Despite a breeze from the lake, the heat under canvas was terrific, and we longed to be under thicker cover; but the dining-room at the mission-house was soon discovered to be just as oppressive. Karema, in fact, resembled a red-hot Brighton; and the surroundings bore so strongly maritime an appearance, that I told Abdullah to go up to the village for water, never dreaming that the boundless supply within twenty yards could be other than salt.

As a matter of fact, the water of Tanganyika is excellent both for cooking and drinking purposes, and proved a great relief after the foul contents of the Ugalla and Ugunda wells. From one of the Fathers we learnt the curious fact that the fort, which is now three-quarters of a mile from the lake, formerly stood on its edge. The waters, it appeared, have receded owing to the breaking down of the bar at the mouth of the Lukugu, which river drains Tanganyika from the opposite side. This dam forms periodically from silted sand and vegetation; causing the level to ascend until the pressure bursts through the accumulation, when a rapid subsidence follows. The cycle of rise and fall is, of course, a phenomenon of many years' extension, probably some fifteen. Captain Stairs discussed the subject with a chief, some fifty-five years of age, who declared that twice in his experience had the waters sunk, and once had they risen. He anticipated that they might be expected to mount again in about two years' time.

Tanganyika abounds in many kinds of beasts, birds, and fishes. On its banks are to be seen the spoor of hippos, antelope, buffalo, and wild boar; still the animals have become very shy in consequence of the increased use of firearms. Lions were also reported to haunt the road; but though we spent several evenings on the look-out, none appeared. By day the waters are covered with wild-fowl of all descriptions, and gulls screamed overhead as in the Red Sea. A small diver with a long beak and grey plumage was frequently to be observed, hovering about fifteen feet above the lake, until some fish was descried, upon which them bird descended with unerring swoop.

The finny race was represented by a kind of sturgeon, pike, and a species not unlike the John Dory. The natives catch them by several clever methods; particularly a sort of lobster-trap large enough to contain a man, and composed of various compartments into which the fish enter, allured by bait. These cages are placed on banks about a mile from the shore, and the hauls are sometimes considerable. Also they use a net about fifteen yards long by two and a half deep, made of bark-fibre, or twine when it can be procured from the coast. This rude seine is weighted with stones at the bottom; and the patient fishermen labour all the night, with nothing but a scanty loin-cloth to protect them from the nipping wind. How they contrive to avoid a capsize in their crazy "dug-outs", which are never properly balanced, seems a mystery to the European. Still accidents seldom occur, and they return at dawn with very fair catches. One evening, as I was walking along the beach, I came across a poor fellow mending his net. There he sat and shivered, a type of the primitive son of toil, with simply an old spear-head for implement. His handiwork nevertheless, would not have shamed Great Yarmouth, either in pace or deftness of knotting.

The approach of the *masika*, or rainy season, was heralded every evening by an easterly wind, which sprang up at sundown and continued until eleven next day. Then it shifted to the north, and blew steadily from that quarter until night began to draw on. The natural conclusion from these warnings was that we should do well to hasten our steps; but unfortunately the transport was by no means calculated to secure a speedy passage.

We had hoped to borrow the steamboat of the London Missionary Society, under charge of Mr. Swann. He, unluckily, was at the south end of the lake, daily expecting the arrival of Mr. H. H. Johnston, the Queen's Commissioner in Nyasaland and so was unable to come to our assistance, unless one of us took charge of his station. This answer, however did not reach Captain Stairs until the 12th, when it was too late to make the Accordingly we had to fall back upon the native dhows and our two small steel boats; with the certainty that the passage of the nineteen miles would occupy a prodigious time. Indeed the start was the reverse of encouraging; since one of the three dhows which put off from Karema on the 10th with No. 3 Company, under the command of the Marquis de Bonchamps, had to return in the night, as she was leaking dangerously. Not only were the vessels old, but their fittings were of the most elementary kind. The body of the dhow consisted merely of the hollowed trunk of some large tree, with a rude stern-post at one end on which to ship the rudder; while another piece of wood, extending from the place where the keel should have been to the gunwale, formed a cut-water. She was rigged with a large triangular sail fitted to a boom, which canvas, when you made a tack, had to be hauled over the top of the mast and lowered on the opposite side. As the dhows could only progress with the wind, a contrary gale might well have detained the expedition for more than a week. In a calm these vexatious craft depended upon paddles plied by a crew of eighteen or twenty. These implements consisted simply of six-foot poles, to which were nailed, for blades, round boards about the size of a saucepan-lid, with loops of cowhide for rowlocks. To put it mildly, neither the style nor the pace of the oarsmen was up to "'Varsity form".

While these lumbering barques were crossing to Mrumbi on the further side, Captain Bodson and I were engaged in putting together the steel boats under a broiling sun. The smaller boat was soon ready; when Captain Stairs tested her on the lake, and returned with a very favourable report. The larger, christened *Blue Nose*, took the greater part of one terrifically hot day; but when finished she appeared a very seaworthy craft, though too long for her beam, and a trifle weak amidships, owing to the absence of transverse bars. On the 13th one of the dhows came back from Mrumbi, after being driven twenty miles to the south by the wind, and then having to depend on her oars for many hours. Captain Bodson promptly went on board with forty loads and twenty-two men, taking with him the small boat with five men, which would row while the calm lasted, and be towed when it came on to blow. A second dhow returned on the following day, and was promptly loaded with forty men and Captain Bodson's donkey. The poor beast was hoisted on board by ten pagazi, and then left on its side with hobbles round the legs. When the third dhow came in she was found capable of containing no loads or donkeys, and only thirty men. Accordingly a considerable detachment still remained in the camp; the further progress of which was delayed by the advent of a stiff gale from the south-west, which rendered all passage impossible.

Tedious though the delay was, it yet had its compensations. On Sunday I went up to the mission chapel for mass, and was much impressed by the size of the building and the orderly demeanour of its large congregation. One of the fathers preached an excellent sermon in Swahili, which the niggers followed with evident interest. They seemed, however, but poor specimens of humanity; and suffered much from malaria, which is prevalent during the rainy season. The children were, many of them, terribly diseased; and the Fathers had an indifferent stock of medicine, owing to the difficulty of communicating with the coast. Luckily small-pox had not made its appearance, though it was reported to be raging on the further side of the lake. As for the women, they seemed a peculiarly slatternly and unwholesome set, wearing next to no clothing, and much addicted both to the smoking and chewing of tobacco. We heard that the mission contemplated a move southward into the British sphere, partly because of the superior climate, and partly from the greater proximity of Nyasaland to civilization and supplies. Besides, in their present position, they were constantly at the mercy of Rumaliza; who had already prevented their settlement in Ujiji, and now threatened their expulsion from Karema.

We dined with the Fathers on several occasions, and had long talks on the best means of suppressing the slave-trade. I cannot say, however, that any of their suggestions seemed particularly feasible; in fact my impression is that, though the Frenchman can make himself fairly comfortable where the Englishman would starve, the former entertains the most rudimentary ideas on the art of government. In writing of the slave-trade, I am reminded that its doughty antagonist, Captain Jacques, arrived from Tabora on the 15th, and paid us a visit next day. His journey seemed to have been a repetition of his earlier experiences; since many of his men deserted, and others had to be left behind from sickness. Again the unfortunate M. Vrithoff had come to fresh mishaps; for while shooting hippos he left open the breech of his Winchester, whereupon the cartridge exploded and nearly blinded him. Captain Jacques also told us that they had bagged eight hippos at Cameron's old camp; and that the Wagunda had made yet another descent upon our old friends at Gongwé, and had at last succeeded in destroying the place by fire.

During these days of waiting, I saw more of Captain Stairs than at any time during the march. One evening I took occasion to examine him, and greatly to my dismay discovered a consolidation of the left lung. The mischief could hardly fail to be increased by a life of continuous exertion and excitement; still, knowing that expostulation would be useless with one of his sanguine temperament, I determined to hold my tongue.

One evening we conversed together at length on the prospects of German East Africa. Captain Stairs, somewhat to my surprise, took an entirely pessimistic view; declaring that Central African trade was worthless from cost of transport, and that a railway to Tanganyika would never return a pennyworth of dividend. He dwelt with much emphasis on the latter point; declaring that none but a lunatic would invest his money in such a concern, and that the undertaking would be tantamount to the casting of millions into the sea.

I remember that at the time these ideas appeared to me unduly sombre; but subsequent reflection entirely confirms he conclusions of Captain Stairs. The development of the territory would be, in any case, no child's play, and the German is entirely raw to colonization. We used to hear a good deal concerning the relative merits of the Wissmann and von Soden systems; but so far as the ordinary intelligence could discover, there was very little method of any kind about the Teutonic administration. Two fundamental ideas seemed to be entertained by such officials as we encountered: the first that ivory was the be-all and end-all of the occupation; and the second that the niggers are best treated as a conquered race, subject, as such, to a war indemnity in the shape of forced contributions. Now the answer to the first theory is, that a State dependent for revenue on ivory must be in a most precarious condition, since not many years hence the supply will cease altogether. Further, that commerce forms a powerful, though indirect encouragement of the slave-trade, since not a tusk is brought to the coast on a free head. As for the military *régime*, the chief objection to it is comprised in the fact that to the crude nigger intelligence it is indistinguishable from robbery.

If a native is deprived of a goat or a fowl, the exaction comes none the sweeter, because effected in the name of the law. The result is that the more timid natives have deserted the road; while the warlike tribes, as the Wagogo and Wahéhé, are ready for indiscriminate reprisals. I observe that, in its recent instructions, the Colonial Department of the German Foreign Office has recommended a more conciliatory procedure on the part of the officials; nor does the injunction come a day too soon. His imperfectly convoluted brain notwithstanding, the nigger draws a distinct line between those that do, and those that do not pay their way.

For general policy the Germans would probably have been well advised to confine themselves in the first instance to the cultivation of the Usagara plateau. It could easily be connected with the coast by a light railway, and would speedily become an African Ceylon. Imported labour, whether coolie or Chinese, would be, however, in my opinion, a *sine qua non*; since the Wasaghara are a miserable race, unintelligent, lazy, and unmuscular. Thence in due course an advance might have been made to the Ugunda plateau, which is suitable alike for pasturage and agriculture. Under the present dispensation the soil remains untouched, and no shiploads of prospective planters disembark at Bagamoyo and Dar-es-Salaam. Possibly the lack of public interest in the German colonies may be in a measure to blame; but I cannot help thinking that the administration spends too much energy upon expeditions and fortifications. Thus resources are exhausted with a surprisingly disappointing result. The garrisons are miserably inadequate, and communications do not exist. When we were at Tabora, the only conclusion possible was that the authorities at Dar-es-Salaam did not care whether Herr von Siegl was dead or alive; since, as I have already mentioned, he had not heard from the coast for three months, and his stock of European provisions cried absolute emptiness. It is only just to say that the road between Tabora and Mpwapwa has since been made secure, by the construction of a station in the Tigogo country. Still, not a single vestige of Teutonic empire exists at Karema, though the position is all-important from the military point of view. It commands the ten days' march to Tabora; and lies but five days' sail from Ujiji, and but ten hours, under favourable conditions, from the west and south sides of Tanganyika. The folly of this neglect will be understood, when it is remembered that Mr. Johnston can deflect the whole of the trade to the bottom of the lake, and thence along the Stevenson road, Nyasa, Shire and Zambesi route, in the interest of the African Lakes Company.

Inland the inefficient supplies of police and soldiery impose little restraint upon the raids of the Masai, the Wadirigo, and the Wahéhé. Still less can any valid control be said to exist over the Arabs, of whom Rumaliza, of Ujiji, may be considered paramount. Indeed the hopelessly impractical policy has been adopted of bullying the weaker chiefs, while the whole fraternity is permitted to import arms and ammunition galore. I am convinced that, though the Kaiser remains a sworn foe to the slave-trade, his representatives in German East Africa entertain mighty little of their master's honourable indignation. Even were they in earnest, the problem possesses tremendous difficulties; were it only from the fact that no single power controls the water-ways, and that one, the Belgian, resembles something very like an imposture. In any case they are entirely mistaken who suppose the Arab, in spite of his burnings and depredations, to be entirely detested by the natives of Central Africa. In the first place he plays a twofold part—that of raider and legitimate middle-man, who satisfies the nigger's keen desire for barter. Even in the former capacity he is careful to keep on amicable terms with powerful and warlike potentates, and to cultivate their good graces by presents and profitable bargains. Through the universal desire for the possession of human chattels he has almost erected himself into a social necessity; and were the big negro kings called upon to chose sides in a life-and-death struggle between Arab and European, the presumption is that they would be found fighting for the former. Again, despite the abominable ferocity of his expeditions, the Arab is a kindly soul; and his courteous treatment of the traveller finds counterpart in his humane conduct towards his slave. Nor is sufficient allowance made, in estimating the effect of his ravages, for the nigger's stoical acquiescence in the inevitable, and happy-go-lucky forgetfulness of past wrongs.

In short the Arab's hold on Africa is far firmer than Exeter Hall imagines; and as he is both ready and willing to fight for his own, the dislodgment cannot be effected as you flick a caterpillar from a wall. Eventually, doubtless, the resources of civilization must triumph over the forces of fanatical barbarism; but the latter contains a deal of staying power, which will try the patience of the European

Governments for several generations, and may not impossibly cause more than one to abandon the contest in despair.

M. de Bonchamps

CHAPTER VIII

MURUNGU

A prayer on Tanganyika—Mount Mrumbi—A dull camp—Captain Joubert's station—Dead donkey—A hostile valley—Rumaliza's Arabs—Our future route—Europeans in Bunkeya?—Alarm of small-pox—The carriers recruited—Farewell to Jacques and Joubert—In the mountains—Makatuba's exploits—A native funeral—The metals of Murungu—Kamba and its foundries—The Kipemba country—Native game-pits—Across the Ludifwa—Thunderstorms—Kassangonwana—A Zanzibari auction—The banks of the Lualaba.

ON the 18th of October the wind shifted at last; and, everything having been placed on board that afternoon, I started next morning at 8.30, with some twenty porters and forty loads. Robinson took over a second detachment in another dhow, but Captain Stairs had to remain behind to finish the business connected with the expedition. The moonlight played on the waters, and the breeze had lulled into a perfect calm. Accordingly the sailors (*baharia*) began to row; but when we had gone a hundred yards from the shore, the captain gave a signal. Instantly the men stopped, blessed themselves, and offered up a prayer (in Swahili) for their safe voyage, again made the sign of the cross, and then fell to their work. No incident in the whole adventure obtained a stronger hold on my imagination; and none save the most phlegmatic could have failed to be profoundly impressed. There I was, a solitary European on a Central African lake; when suddenly the stillness of the night was broken by voices praying in one's own religion. A sense of common hopes and interests came over the mind, and the civilization of the Dark Continent appeared less of a dream than usual.

Robinson's boat came level during the night with her sail hoisted. Both crews promptly shouted themselves hoarse, and began to row with all their might, until we raised our canvas and gave the other dhow the good-bye. At daylight, about 5.30 a.m., we reached the west side of Tanganyika, about four miles to the south of Mount

Mrumbi; but were obliged to put off again as the natives, about a hundred strong, made hostile demonstrations, and showed every disposition to dispute our lauding. Accordingly we rowed to a creek near the camping-ground selected by M. de Bonchamps, and disembarked with the assistance of Captain Bodson. On the way to camp I met the Marquis, who gave me a most animated account of his passage with No. 3 Company. I have already mentioned that one dhow had to return leaking at every pore; well, the second nearly sank several times, broke her helm, and had to take refuge in a small bay while repairs were being effected. The wind tore the sail of the third boat, and compelled her to make for the shore; during which process she fouled a sleeping hippo, who resented the unintended insult by taking a piece from her side. However, all ended happily; and Bonchamps had employed his spare time in drilling the men, and with excellent results, though the talking in the ranks would have given a British sergeant-major convulsions.

The camp seemed unhealthy, and was certainly overpoweringly hot. Midges swarmed in the tents, and a general feeling of limpness seemed to have taken possession of the white men. Captain Bodson and I made an attempt in the *Blue Nose* to shoot hippos and crocodile, but without success. We rowed for five miles, but could not bag a single specimen; though the shore was covered with their marks, notably the half-circle made by the tail, when they get into position facing the water. The reptiles, unfortunately for us, had too keen a sight, and slipped into the lake when we were quite a hundred yards off. Accordingly we had to content ourselves with examining the rock formations, which lay in three layers of granite, slag, and earth. Altogether we voted Mrumbi the dreariest camp we had occupied during the whole expedition. Little to do by day; and at night time continuous thunderstorms—forewarnings, of course, of the *masika*—which prevented sleep, more especially when both boys and cook had to be accommodated inside one's tent, as their grass huts would not keep out the rain. On the 21st a dhow arrived with forty men, and two more next day, which completed our complement; accordingly Captain Jacques' caravan began to cross. Then the wind shifted northward, and detained Captain Stairs until he was many days overdue.

I turned donkey-doctor during the interval; as both Captain Stairs' and Captain Bodson's beasts had been grievously injured in the fetlocks, during passage of the lake, owing to clumsy stowage. The former had been purchased from the missionaries at Karema, and was a capital galloper, able, also, to jump like a deer. Unfortunately, both of them had been so terribly knocked about, that medical aid proved futile, and they had to be shot. My animal, which had come all the way from Bagamoyo, was now one of the two survivors.

About a mile from our camp lay the station of St. Louis Mrumbi, built by Captain Joubert, of the Belgian Anti-Slavery Society. He was of French nationality, and had originally served in the Papal Zouaves, whence he passed into the Society's employment about the year 1880, and had been on his present mission for about a twelvemonth. He came into camp soon after our arrival; and appeared to be about forty-five years of age, short, but very sturdily built. His station had been erected upon a spur of the mountain, about three hundred yards by sixty; and commanded a little plain, covered with native villages. The cloud-capped summit of Mrumbi rose some six miles off, to a height of some five thousand feet above the level of the lake. The actual peak ascended almost square from the shoulders, and was flat-topped, like most of its neighbours. It was absolutely destitute of vegetation, and seemed composed of some reddish stone. Mrumbi was, however, hidden from the view of the fort by intervening crags; and the whole country appeared broken into rocks and ravines, while below lay the blue waters of Tanganyika. The spot was extremely picturesque, and appeared to have been selected with a keen eye to defensive purposes. Captain Joubert had surrounded his village with a brick wall fourteen feet high and two and a half thick; while a short distance off, separated by a deep gully, stood a second city of refuge, comprising his house and barracks, surrounded by a another wall. Close at hand he had built a chapel, capable of holding about two hundred people, with a sacristy and sleeping-room at the back for Father Van Oost, a Belgian, who used to come for service from the Mpala mission, about a day's journey to the north. We saw one of these worthy priests, who took charge of two dhows which had been lent to the Jacques caravan. He informed me that Tanganyika owns a private sea-serpent some thirty feet long, and that he had seen it twice; on one occasion swimming in the water, and on the second sleeping on the shore. After the description of this tremendous reptile, we were glad to have to deal with none more formidable than whip-snakes, about a yard in length, but reputed to be very dangerous.

Captain Joubert's supply of medicine was almost exhausted; and I readily consented to attend some sick men among his small garrison of two hundred Zanzibaris, Wanyamwesi, and natives recruited from the neighbourhood. Still more serious was his deficiency in rifles, owing to the non-arrival of a consignment despatched by way of Quilimane. His actual supply consisted of a most miscellaneous assortment of chassepots, Remingtons, and muzzle-loaders, without suitable cartridges. He was compelled, therefore, to act on the strict defensive against the very bellicose natives in the valley below; indeed, one of his soldiers had been speared two days before our arrival without any seeming provocation. Fortunately the approach of two such large expeditions as our own and Captain Jacques' alarmed his most turbulent neighbour, Katélé, a chief living about three miles south; and the latter evacuated the country bag and baggage. Still there remained within uncomfortably close quarters a sufficiently unruly set. They resembled the Wagogo not a little, both in their arms and disdain for clothing—contenting themselves with a small piece of cloth in front and a slightly larger piece behind—and marched into our camp in the same lordly fashion; though they were ready enough to trade in goats, flour, and wood. We noticed that their teeth were all filed, and the majority shaved their heads in the most elaborate fashion. Some bared both sides, leaving a band of hair on the skull; others wore only a small tuft on its apex; and an arrangement of ridge and furrow was also fashionable. Also a certain number did not shave at all, but wore their locks long, and plaited with string, so as to produce the appearance of a multitude of tails. Their villages, containing altogether some six thousand inhabitants, consisted of circular huts without any stockade. In these, children and adults herded in the most promiscuous fashion, though some of the grandees rejoiced in a sleeping- mat. They appeared strangely ignorant of the outside world, owing to the isolation of the valley from the usual caravan routes; which either cross the lake from Ujiji to the north of Mpala, or skirt the north coast and so reach the Manyuema country.

Captain Joubert's most inveterate enemies were, however, the emissaries of Rumaliza. That sheikh had sworn to have his blood; and his slaves had for months been enlisting an army of *ruga-ruga* and other rapscallions to wipe him out. They were in active alliance with Katélé; and had constructed an extended camp about twelve miles from St. Louis, as a basis of operations. Luckily they also took the alarm, and thought it advisable to retreat across the lake to Ujiji. Next day Captain Joubert's men visited the spot, and found nothing except a little child, half-starved, who had been shut in a large wicker-work bin and left to her fate. The pressure was therefore renewed for the time being; and Captain Joubert, reinforced by Captain Jacques, was able to make his position very fairly secure. The latter had brought him a commission as officer of the Congo Free State; and he promptly proceeded to send the flag to various kings in Urua, and to Mpweto, a potentate dwelling to the north of Lake Mweru. As we proposed to descend by a somewhat circuitous route upon Mpweto's kingdom, I asked Captain Joubert if we should not have done better to cross from Karema to Mriro, or some landing-place further south. He answered "No", since our proposed way, though longer, was less mountainous and less destitute of provisions and water. This sounded cheerful; though, as a matter of fact, the journey through Murungu proved quite hilly enough for our taste, and food, from causes which I shall afterwards mention, none too plentiful.

On the 28th a rumour went the round of the camp that Captain Stairs' boat was in sight; but the strongest binoculars failed to reveal its presence, which existed only in some active Zanzibari imagination. Next day, however, he did actually arrive, after a crossing of soma thirty-six hours; and promptly gave orders for a start on Saturday (the 31st). There were special reasons why we should hasten our steps, because a report had reached St. Louis of the presence of two Englishmen in Bunkeya. "Manicaland over again," was the general comment; and I was informed, though not by Captain Stairs himself, that King Leopold's instructions ran as follows: If our expedition arrived first upon the debateable ground, we should warn off our filibustering compatriots, and, if necessary, use force for their ejection; if, however, we had been forestalled, a passive attitude was to be adopted, pending an appeal to Europe. As matters turned out, the alleged Britons resolved themselves into peaceful missionaries; still, a mythical Mr. Joseph Thomson exercised a very real momentum upon the third, or Mrumbi-Bunkeya stage, of our pilgrimage.

A wild alarm of small-pox in camp was the chief incident of our last days at Mrumbi. Now, the epidemic raged through the plain; and as our men had been in and out of the different villages to buy food, infection seemed both possible and probable. However, the supposed case was found on examination to be nothing more than a rash produced by the sun, and Captain Stairs' anxieties were soon set at rest. Afterwards two porters did actually sicken of the disease, but it assumed a mild form and they both recovered.

We had enlisted forty-five natives to carry loads to Lake Mweru; and sturdy barbarians they were, well set-up and muscular about the loins. They were, however, totally unused to the work, and performed their parts very indifferently. Their arrival was certainly opportune, as one or two men had recently deserted, and others had fallen sick. However; a rearrangement of the caravan seemed necessary, as there was a deficiency in askari; and some of the Zanzibari pagazi were promoted to the superior position. Accordingly a general shuffling ensued, in which each officer appeared most desirous to rid his company of its lazier members. The Marquis do Bonchamps, in particular, was most anxious that I should take over a most notorious shirker; who, as he ingenuously explained, would be compelled to work if a boat-section fell to his lot. Captain Stairs, however, frustrated the little plan, and after some confusion the safari started on its third and final stage.

On our way to Fort St. Louis, my donkey fell dead lame; so there was nothing for it but to take off the saddle and bridle, and hand him over to Captain Joubert who, with Captain Jacques, was waiting to see us off. The latter brought his camera to bear upon the boats; and promised me copies of that, and the one hundred and fifty other photographs he had taken, if we both returned to Europe. There was a deal of virtue in that "if", for it would have been futile to deny that the two brave men were left in anything but an easy position.

Their chief source of strength lay in their cordial co-operation; Joubert having chivalrously acquiesced in the arrangement, whereby Captain Jacques should assume supreme command, while they should administer separate districts, the former with headquarters at St. Louis, the latter at Albertville. Again the pair formed a sufficiently harmonious blend: Jacques' courage, which was not far removed from rashness, being counter-balanced by Joubert's caution and experience. (As a matter of fact, Captain Jacques appears to have precipitated events by setting Rumaliza at defiance, when a more conciliatory bearing might have delayed the crisis.) Still, the moral effect of our temporary halt at St. Louis would soon evaporate; and so inveterate an enemy as the Arab would speedily discover the Belgians' lamentable deficiency in munitions of war. Indeed the latest intelligence (I am writing in January, 1893), is that they have sustained a grave reverse, in spite of the most fortunate arrival to the rescue of M. Delcommune. Speculation appears unnecessary just now; because, by the time that these lines are in print, we shall probably possess full details of their vicissitudes and ultimate fate. The fact remains that, whether reinforcements save the situation or not, they were left for over a twelvemonth, face to face with a fanatical and unscrupulous foe, with little powder, and a stock of rifles which might have been furnished by the armoury of some provincial theatre. No more pertinent illustration could be desired of the folly—I had almost set down criminality—of founding empires "on the cheap".

A steep ascent for over two hours made the sweat run off the men like rain, and next day the road offered even greater difficulties, huge boulders alternating with nearly perpendicular rises. The eye was delighted with the wild variety of cliff and chasm; but it was cruel work for the porters, more especially when a heavy thunderstorm caused the rocks to become slippery as ice. The poor fellows fell flat on their backs, while the loads descended on their chests, and in several instances serious injuries ensued to ribs and breasts. Still there were humorous incidents in plenty, particularly when we arrived at a stream thirty feet wide, and crossed by a crazy bridge of poles. In order to expedite matters, Captain Stairs ordered me to ford the current with the boats at a crossing some fifty yards lower down. The unfamiliar element created an absolute panic among the pagazi; they had to be driven into the water; and, though it was barely waist-deep, I was forced to rush in post-haste, as one hulking chap dropped his section in sheer terror. Again, our solitary donkey unshipped her load near a village, without which stood the usual groups of curious natives. Straightway the askari threw down their guns and ran to pick it up, in entire forgetfulness of the fact that, had the niggers been malevolently disposed, they might have speared us at their leisure.

A half-caste slave-dealer, Makatuba by name, the slave of a rich merchant at Zanzibar, had passed through this land of Murungu some months previously, and signs of his devastating progress were seen at every turn. Thus we encamped on the 4th of November on the site of a large village which the miscreant had burnt, and on the opposite hill stood the charred ruins of several more. In the course of a day's march we passed no less than five absolutely deserted, since their men had been massacred, and the women arid children carried into captivity. These tokens of malignant destruction exercised a profound influence upon the impressionable pagazi. They huddled over the fires by night, and talked in whispers, contrary to their usual habit of sustaining conversation in ear-splitting key. Their consternation increased when we passed within a few miles of the scoundrel's permanent camp, though, fortunately enough, he made no sign.

One night, as we were encamped under the depressing circumstances of rain, cold, and half- rations caused by Makatuba's ravages, a native shouted from the opposite hill, "Who are you; are you Arabs?" Our guide replied, "Our chiefs are *Ingreze* (Englishmen), who travel peacefully through the country." A nyampara and two askaris were sent out to assure the man of our pacific intentions; and the result appeared next day, when a band of fire-eaters came into camp, and requested Captain Stairs to shoot some neighbours with whom they had a quarrel. They appeared infinitely disgusted when he declined to accede to their request. Indeed, for all Makatuba's atrocities, the inhabitants of Murungu found time for plenty of fighting among themselves. One day we were startled by the noise of a fusillade; which we discovered to proceed from a party, who were firing a funeral salute over a comrade's grave. He had been shot in the arm, while asleep, by a poisoned arrow; and though the wound was a mere scratch, he died within six hours. Captain Stairs kindly gave me the head, which I still possess, and it was covered with a paste of vegetable poison.

On the 8th we crossed the Lufuko, a river some thirty yards wide, and nine feet deep, which flows into Tanganyika above Mpala; and left the mountains behind us. Mightily glad we were, for the porters had been terribly tried, and besides the two with cases of small-pox, I had several invalids, one of whom a poor chap, named Banga Baloze, succumbed to fever and general exhaustion, though we carried him for several days. On more than one occasion the porters were obliged to go supperless to bed, and latterly we made forced marches to get out of the sandy and inhospitable *pori*. In spite of its repellent features, the country of Murungu, and more especially the Makololo range to the south, will probably become a source of wealth to future generations of Europeans. There can be little doubt, I imagine, that the rocks are peculiarly rich in minerals. About two hours to the south of Mount Mrumbi, on the shore of Tanganyika, lies a spot whence the natives extract copper and gold-dust. Captain Joubert had visited the mines, and he told us that the vein seemed to have been worked with considerable skill. According to him, it appeared to go some distance inland, and then came to a sudden stop. The natives sold him a copper ingot, and some specimens of a metal resembling malachite, which they professed to have dug out of the adjacent cliffs. Also it appeared that Rumaliza's men had been prospecting in the neighbourhood, though they abandoned the quest without any substantial result. Captain Stairs was most anxious to examine the deposits; but the passage of the lake had consumed such an inordinate time, that he could not afford the three or four days' delay, which a thorough investigation would have entailed.

However, at Kaomba, where we halted on the 3rd of November, the signs, not indeed of copper, but of iron, were unmistakable. The metal exists in considerable quantities and in a pure condition, especially under the form of red haematite. Hence the village is famed far and wide for its foundries, in which hoes, axes, and spear-heads are fashioned.

Unfortunately the evening came on so squally, that zeal for information gave way to a carnal longing for the camp-fire, and none of us paid those interesting buildings the attention they deserved. I can but vaguely remember several edifices with high conical roofs; in the centre of which were pits about eighteen feet by six and shallower at one end than the other. The furnace was constructed of clay; and the blast appeared to be produced by bellows, some twenty in number, composed of two parallel wooden tubes fitting into one nozzle, which was smeared with clay so as to keep off the fire. These pipes were worked by sticks held in either hand, and moved rapidly up and down upon some principle of suction which I, unhappily, "took for granted", as did the proverbial American tourist the

Coliseum. However, I can distinctly recall the low open sheds which formed the smithies, with their stone anvils and hammers, the last devoid of handles. There the smelted iron was made into implements, or into the masses weighing from two pounds to two and a half, in which it is carried about for sale. These lumps are shaped like a very fat cigar, with a small rod projecting from either end. As for the hoes and spears, they appear rude to the eye accustomed to the products of Sheffield. At the same time their balance is admirable; and though a European carpenter would throw aside a Murungu axe with disdain, a native contrives therewith to cut, or rather dig, through a thick tree- trunk in a marvellously short space of time.

The Lufuko may be considered to form the western boundary of Murungu; for the intermediate district between that river and the Ludifwa, though assigned to Murungu in the maps, is known to the natives as the Kipemba country. The first marches were through swamps, varied by small streams; and the vegetation consisted chiefly of dwarf bamboo, though the more open spaces were covered with herbage and flowers. It was no easy matter to get the caravan along, as the porters stuck in the marsh, and blocks occurred at every little bridge. In the valley of the Lufuko we traversed several forests whose trees, of hard close-grained timber, would form excellent material for the construction of canoes. Some of them were covered with a round fruit about the size of a plum, with a bitter skin leaving a taste as of tannin in the mouth, but containing four triangular kernels of a peculiarly sweet flavour. The pagazi, on spying this delicacy, threw down their loads and rushed madly at the branches. In some places the trees were packed together in a manner to be seen only in the tropics; and the masses of timber, creepers, and ferns reminded Captain Stairs of the Aruwhimi country traversed by the Emin Relief Expedition. The beautiful vistas had been entirely depopulated by Makatuba, and for five days we did not pass a single inhabited village. On the 9th, however, we lighted upon a retired colony, which had somehow escaped the fiend's ravages. The people exhibited every sign of friendship, when they discovered that we had no connection with their terrible enemy, and came readily into camp. They were a fine and intelligent race; and though the men smeared their hair with an evil-smelling mixture of red clay and grease, the ladies dressed their frizzy locks with beads of various colours—pink being the favourite—which showed a distinct niceness of taste.

These people are ardent hunters; and pursue buffalo and antelope in large parties, frequently armed with muzzle-loaders. Their favourite device for supplying their larders is, however, that of game-pits. These traps are dug in a pathway about a quarter of a mile long, say, by thirty feet wide. They are about four feet by ten, and perhaps twenty in number; being so disposed, moreover, that if the beast escapes the first, he is bound to be entrapped by the second or third. Within the pits are planted sharp stakes, and then the top is covered with small boughs overlaid with grass and earth. The whole village assembles to the signal of a drum, and the frightened animals, deer, buffalo, and frequently the mighty elephant, are driven in the desired direction; the plain being frequently fired as an additional element of terror. So ingeniously are these snares contrived, that they sometimes bring confusion upon the unwary traveller; and I remember that Captain Stairs narrowly escaped a nasty fall into one of them while gathering botanical specimens.

The Lufuko is separated from the Ludifwa by a small range of hills; and on the 10th of November we crossed the latter stream, which runs into the Lufunso, and so into the Lualaba. The tracks of elephants were frequently to be seen in the bamboo- beds; but the beasts had become so shy from the constant pursuit of Arab and Wanyamwesi hunters, that we never got so much as a shot. About a march or so from the Ludifwa we entered fine undulating prairie-land, capable of supporting any amount of sheep and cattle. The plateau, from its height above the sea, would be inhabitable by a European population; and while the highlands would form excellent pasturage, the valleys, with their thick beds of vegetable mould, would grow rice and all the vegetables produced by the natives, as manioc, maize, and *matamah*. In fact, Kipenbaland way will become, a generation or two hence, an African Bengal; more especially as irrigation will be rendered unnecessary by the numerous streams of fresh clear water which, according to the natives, remain unexhausted in the dry season.

The chief drawbacks to our enjoyment were the scarcity of provisions—for with the exception of two antelope shot by the Marquis de Bonchamps, we bagged no game—and the thunderstorms, which came on without the slightest notice, and frequently put out every fire in the camp, greatly to the suffering of the poor porters. On these occasions the lightning used to play about the tents in a decidedly awesome fashion; and the wind swept the earth with such vehemence that the boys had to hold, for dear life, to poles and canvas, otherwise the whole structure would have been blown away. After an hour's turmoil the storm suddenly dropped; and by the light of the revisible moon—for these visitations generally occurred at or after sunset—you could see the shivering pagazi painfully endeavouring to rekindle their fires with the damp wood.

After a most uncomfortable experience of the sort, we were glad to halt for a day at the village of Pakasukamara, to engage porters, instead of the Murungu men, who would travel no further with us from fear of Msiri. The chief of the district, a burly youth, Kassongonwana by name, professed to be nephew of the Katanga potentate, and certainly bore the Wanyamwesi tribal marks, the filed teeth, and so forth. He was not, however, on the best of terms with his uncle; and proclaimed that, with Captain Stairs' assistance, he was ready to take the field against the despot at a moment's notice. This obliging offer was, much to his annoyance, declined with thanks; he accepted, however, the Belgian flag which Captain Stairs hoisted over the village that afternoon, November the 11th. The standard was also received by the powerful sultan, Katumba, who had quitted this neighbourhood three years previously, after a fracas with Kassongonwana, and established himself some twelve miles distant on the banks of the Lualaba.

Our nyamparas turned the idle day into account by holding a Petticoat Lane fair, in which garments changed hands at enormous prices. Abdullah, who paid much attention to the adornment of his person, purchased a gaudily striped shirt for five rupees, or six shillings. It would have been unkind to damp his pride by the information that the article would not have fetched more than tenpence or a shilling in England; arid I must own that fabrics were dear in Central Africa. Thus we were told that across the Lualaba a *shukkah* (two yards) of American cloth sold for quite sixteen rupees.

On the 13th we crossed a small swamp, traversed some hilly meadow-land, with grass up to the knee, forded a stream about twenty feet wide, and so descended on the Lufunso, a tributary of the Lualaba. On my arrival with the rear-guard, I found Captain Stairs directing the crossing of the safari. The current ran very fast, and the water was waist-deep in parts, and thirty yards wide. Nevertheless, the passage was accomplished with singularly few mishaps, by the following arrangement. A rope was thrown across the river from the east bank, and attached to a tree at the near end, while, on the opposite side, a string of askari kept it taut. About twenty yards out another rope was fastened to this line, and, being fastened to a trunk which overhung the stream some distance off, acted as a stay. The pagazi entered the water one by one on the lower side of this contrivance, with their loads on their heads, and with one hand grasping the longer rope. Most of them got across without a ducking; but now and again you would witness the disappearance of some luckless individual, burden, gun, and all. The askari, however, came to the rescue with business-like promptitude; picked up the load, and replaced it on the pate of the spluttering wretch.

Finally, the last man on the east side of the Lufunso untied the shorter rope; looped it to the longer; and doubled the two round an over hanging bough, whence, as soon as he was safely across, it was detached by a smart jerk from the askari.

That night we encamped by the broad Lualaba, which separated us from Urua, and Katanga, the goal of all our efforts. The sun set beyond the lofty range of mountains; which, with their steep peaks clothed to the summits with trees, formed an imposing background to a scene of extended magnificence and variety.

CHAPTER IX

ACROSS THE LUALABA

Character of the Lualaba — Kafindo's account—The fords — Ngwena's visit—Our message to Msiri—The Lufunso—A *shauri* between Ngwena and Mpweto—The medicine-man—Holiness under eclipse—Passage of the Lualaba—The Urua mountains — Buffaloes — Robinson's sufferings— The plain of Chewella—Kafindo—Uturutu—Zanzibari philosophy—A domestic tragedy—The Belgian flag distributed—Malagarazi—Famine ahead—The Luvua and Lufira—The Lukulwe—M. Legat and escort—His views on the situation—Bia and Delcommune—Bunkeya at last.

THE point at which the Stairs expedition hit the Lualaba, was at latitude 8° 09' 44" south, and longitude 29° 06' 45"east, and about fifteen miles, or two short marches north of Lake Mweru. Nearly three-quarters of a mile from camp, the Lufunso discharged its waters into the main stream; and very deep they were, abounding, moreover, in crocodiles and fish. As for the Lualaba, though very wide—the distance from bank to bank must have been quite half, and, in some places, nearly a mile—the first impression, that of a profound volume of water, proved wholly illusory. Captain Stairs took several soundings; and established the fact that, though the river was nearly thirty feet deep in parts, yet, barely a boat's length away, sharp dentated rocks were to be found within a very little of the surface. Fords were numerous, and the experienced hand could cross without getting wet above the waist. In no place did the Lualaba appear navigable, except to canoes of the shallowest draught. Again, some two and a half miles upstream, the channel, after a wide sweep to the west, became impeded by numerous wooded islands; and beyond them again could be descried the angry foam of rapids, quite three-fourths of a mile wide, among which a stranger would be shipwrecked to a certainty. The natives told us that only one opening was navigable, except in the month of January; and we afterwards learnt from the Arab Kafindo that, further north, the river was equally inhospitable.

According to that distinctly intelligent personage, the Lualaba, for seven long marches, tumbles over its rocky bed in a constant succession of rapids, varied by two considerable cataracts. The statement seems credible enough, when one considers that at our camp the stream was three thousand feet above the sea level; and at Nyangwé, where Commander Cameron crossed, its height can only be reckoned at two thousand three hundred feet. Now, the latter place lies about four hundred miles to the north, so that the drop must be over a foot and a half to the mile. As to the subsequent course of the Lualaba, the Arab was hardly explicit in detail, though his general views were stated with precision. He held that fifteen marches to the north-north-west of our camp the river joins Msiri's Lualaba, otherwise known as the Kamolundo; and that this united stream, yet five marches further on, meets the Lukugu, flowing from Lake Tanganyika. If this theory becomes established by subsequent discovery, it will redound greatly to the credit of Commander Cameron, who came to much the same conclusion nearly twenty years ago.

Not only is the Lualaba a shallow stream, but its rise in the rainy season is very small compared with most African rivers. Thus, the natives told us, that fords which in summer time are only waist-deep, do not immerse the body above the chest, even in the month of January. This slight difference in level seems the more remarkable, because both in Kipemba and Murungu it rains for five months in the year; and so great is the downpour, that the inhabitants can only grow one harvest. Also, there are no prevailing winds, as the north-east and south-east monsoon, which blow on the west coast and inland as far as Tanganyika.

The potentate of the district, Ngwena by name, dwelt on an island, which was approached by a ford, about a quarter of a mile from the camp. He was a declared enemy of Msiri, on whom, indeed, he had inflicted more than one reverse, though he had finally thought it good policy to retire from the mainland. We soon heard that he was going to pay us a visit; and, on the morning of the 14th of November, his regal form was perceived being borne across the river. Ngwena was a slight, shrivelled-up old gentleman, with European features and a skin of light copper-colour. He was attired in a dark-blue calico sheet, which had seen many winters but few washings. His intentions, however, were amiability itself; and, while complaining, not without reason, of hard times, he brought a small present of honey and eggs. Also, he promised us boats for crossing the river, and in due season kept his word. But his general policy appeared decidedly vacillating. He was delighted to hear that we had come to suppress Msiri's barbarities, and yet seemed to look upon them as part of the natural scheme of things.

On the Lualaba we halted for a week (November 13th to 19th), and the rest did the men a deal of good. Latterly we had been compelled to leave a considerable number behind in the villages to recover from weakness. Bedoe, the head chief, was rallying from a severe attack of illness, and all the white men showed signs of wear and tear. The real reason for the delay, however, was to give our messengers time to get to Bunkeya, and to rejoin us with Msiri's answer at some village a respectful distance from the capital. The embassy consisted of the chief Massoudi, an intelligent and trustworthy man, with four askaris; and it bore a letter signed "Stairs, the Englishman", which announced our impending arrival, and the amicable nature of our intentions. Massoudi also carried with him a large present of cloth, to conciliate the avaricious king. He left camp on the morning of the 14th, and thus received five days' start.

Our time was chiefly spent in vain attempts to get a shot at hippos, and in equally unsuccessful efforts to catch fish on the Lufunso. That river swarmed with a species of trout, barbel, and a sucking fish, which lives upon the solid matter drawn into its round mouth from the water. They were, however, so completely glutted with food that none of us could get a rise; though Captain Stairs, for one, tried repeatedly. Nets, night-lines, spoon-bait, and artificial flies proved equally inefficient; and the clearness of the river made the occupation all the more tantalizing, as you could see the fishes playing practical jokes with the hook. One evening, while thus engaged, I was fortunate enough to secure a very different kind of victim. On the opposite bank a leopard began to call, and was soon joined by his mate, with whom he began to play. My askari promptly produced a gun and I shot the male. He gave a bound, looked about him in absolute amazement, and then fell stone dead. Still the female could not realize the situation, and as she stood sniffing at her companion, a second barrel finished the business. Next morning a boat was procured from Ngwena's, and the skins of the pair soon hung in my tent. Also we drilled the pagazi now and then, but the novelty of that discipline had already worn off and they displayed very little of the alacrity, which was conspicuous at Mount Mrumbi. One morning Captain Bodson and I went up the Lualaba towards Lake Mweru after duck. In that respect we were much disappointed; but the excursion was rewarded, some five miles from camp, by the discovery of a cataract quite a mile across, succeeded by two miles of breakers raging over the rocks. The fall was not very high, still, so far as the eye could see, the waters were covered with turbulent foam, and their roar could be heard quite a mile away. We arrived in camp just in time to assist at a *shauri*, or palaver, between Ngwena and Mpweto, a king who, as I have already mentioned, rules a large district containing some fifteen villages on the shore of Lake Mweru. Their quarrel had been of old standing, and Captain Stairs, in the interests of peace, had undertaken to act as mediator. Accordingly we seated ourselves in a row; one of our chiefs who knew the Mweru dialect, prepared to act as interpreter; and the litigants were admitted. It must be confessed that poor old Ngwena cut a sorry figure beside his antagonist, a fine burly fellow, with a jet black skin, and his head adorned by a roll of human hair and fibre. Moreover, Ngwena had with him only twenty attendants, all somewhat undersized, and armed with spears; whereas Mpweto was accompanied by fifty stalwart warriors equipped with muzzle-loaders or bows with poisoned arrows. The latter body advanced with military precision, until they arrived before our seats. Then they laid their guns on the ground, clapped hands, picked up the weapons again, and squatted alongside of their king and over against Ngwena's train. Next to Mpweto stood his medicine- man, who presented a most extraordinary figure. He was a tall individual, bent with age, and from his countenance, which was plastered with white clay, projected an enormous Roman nose, rivalling the Duke of Wellington's in size. Round his forehead ran a band of leopard's skin, ornamented with cowries and stuck full of feathers; while about his person hung rams' horns, which he used for cupping, and various charms against snake-bites or accidents, which he sold at exorbitant prices. The most potent of these were empty revolver cartridges, a noted specific throughout Central Africa.

The controversy was amusing at first, but eventually became terribly wearisome. A goat, it appeared, had been the original subject of contention, whence had developed diplomatic variance, terminating in raids and regular warfare. In vain did Ngwena attempt to show that Mpweto must have been a mere child at the time of the original *casus belli*. "Yes," was the crushing reply, "you are indeed an aged man, and your memory is fast leaving you." Whereupon Mpweto's warriors grunted applause, and his rival waxed exceeding wroth. After the wrangle had raged for an hour and more, the medicine-man attempted to give his version of the story, but the prospect of a third disputant was altogether too much for Captain Stairs. "Tell the old fool," he said to the interpreter, "he had better be silent, or I will turn him out of camp." Mpweto looked absolutely aghast at this cavalier treatment of his chancellor and high-priest; but the medicine-man collapsed, and Captain Stairs eventually settled the quarrel on the basis of *uti possidetis*. The two kings went off together to Ngwena's village, there to hold a festival of reconciliation; the medicine-man professed to repair to the woods for a night of prayer. Yet a malicious rumour traversed the camp next day that the saint, having partaken to excess of pombé, had been observed making uncertain tacks towards the doorway of a hut, whence he did not emerge until the sun was high. Be that as it may, his temporal lord reappeared next morning none the worse for his potations, and went off in high good humour after a second *shauri*, at which be accepted the Belgian flag. Old Ngwena followed suit; though the morrow had brought apprehensions of Mpweto's capacities for renewed mischief, which were hardly allayed by the ceremony.

On the 19th the passage of the Lualaba was effected in the steel boats, which carried the loads, and ten canoes lent by Ngwena, wherein sat the pagazi. Thanks to the discipline established by Captain Stairs; the operation took wonderfully little time, and in two hours and twenty-five minutes every man was across. From the river we ascended a spur of the Urua mountains; and made, in addition, long marches of fourteen miles a day. The chief novelty was the enormous quantity of buffalo frequenting the wooded slopes, and those of the dangerous kind known as the Cape species. One morning, just after we had set out, I was startled by a regular fusillade, and imagined that the natives must have attacked the caravan. However, on reaching the spot with the askari, I discovered the enemy to be an enormous bull, into whom the Marquis de Bonchamps was pouring lead. The unwieldy beast made several charges, but he had fortunately been crippled by a shot early in the encounter, and eventually fell, game to the last. The men, who were on half-rations, appreciated his beef; but I am bound to say that the steak which fell to my share proved absolutely uneatable from toughness. Next day the caravan emerged with less credit from a meeting with a cow and her calf. She came crashing through the underwood, and ran to the left of the line. Captain Stairs thereupon fired, but missed, owing to the thickness of the jungle. The beast, after going about two hundred yards away from our rear, suddenly wheeled round, charged the caravan with her head down and her little eyes twinkling wickedly, and then disappeared in the forest. The porters, it is needless to say, had resorted to their usual tactics—loads were flung to earth, guns hurled anywhither, and the neighbouring trees presented a dissolving view of ascending arms and legs. In due course their spirits recovered, and the monotonous tramp continued without further stampedes.

In some respects this portion of the journey was not unpleasant, since the rain held off, and we had well-water in abundance. Still fever was rife in the camp; and it laid hold of the Marquis de Bonchamps and several of the chiefs, including Hamadi. Poor Robinson was a most melancholy spectacle, since, by way of variety to his troubles, the soles of his feet had become violently inflamed. As there was no donkey for him to ride, he was compelled to hobble along, bent nearly double, and each step must have caused him positive agony. None of us had particularly pleasant experiences on the Stairs expedition, but I am inclined to think that Robinson endured the most actual suffering. Nevertheless his pluck continued entirely unabated, and he stuck to his work without a word of complaint.

On the 22nd and 23rd we marched along the Luvule, which joins the Lualaba between Ngwena's and Mpweto's on Lake Mweru. Then we crossed a stretch of mountainous and wooded country, succeeded by plateaux, watered by the tributaries of the Luvua. In the valleys lay the oozes or bogs of which Livingstone speaks, and on one of them, known as the plain of Chewella, we had some excellent sport. The whole face of the meadow was alive with buffalo and antelope, the latter being of the sort called the Vardoni. They stand about three and a half feet at the shoulder, and are of a reddish colour with a long coat and lyre-shaped horns. We could see them bounding over the plain in large herds, and following their leader like a flock of sheep. No sooner was the camp pitched than we all turned out, though Robinson went off to his tent after a shot or two. Captain Stairs opened fire at five hundred yards, but soon came to closer quarters; near him walked the Marquis at a furious rate, then came Captain Bodson, and last myself. The game streamed past in magnificent array, and the rifle-shots rang out continuously. Presently the lines of fire crossed; and the Marquis de Bonchamps' bullets, coming unpleasantly near, forced Captain Stairs and myself to take refuge behind some ant-hills, until his attention was attracted by the frantic waving of our helmets. The antelope were not easy to kill; though out of eighteen wounded I managed to secure four, including a splendid buck, the king of a herd. My first shot hit him in the head, when he made off with a tremendous plunge. The movement showed that the bullet had not miscarried, and shortly afterwards I came up to him as he stood facing me and surrounded by his wives. The second shot caught him in the chest; but he was still able to stagger about forty yards, when he suddenly stopped, turned a complete somersault, and then lay motionless on his back with his horns buried in the soil. When we came to count the head, Captain Stairs had shot two, Captain Bodson five, and the Marquis one antelope and one buffalo. Later in the afternoon Captain Bodson went out again and bagged four more, so that the Zanzibaris were able to gorge themselves to their hearts content, and thus realized their maximum of happiness. The plain of Chewella, however, appeared in a very different character next day; for a violent thunderstorm converted it into an absolute swamp, and though we carefully skirted the edge, falls were numerous upon the slippery foothold.

  From Ngwena's, Captain Stairs had despatched our nyampara, Khamis Ngozi, on an embassy to Kafindo, one of the most notorious raiders of the country of Urua. He came into camp the evening before we crossed the Lualaba; and courteously promised to catch us up in a day or two rather than delay the passage. From time to time messengers arrived, announcing his arrival on the following day; but his notions of keeping an appointment lacked definiteness, and Captain Stairs made more than one halt in expectation of his appearance. At last, when we had abandoned all hope, his escort of thirty-five Zanzibaris, Wanyamwesi, and Warua recruits was descried in our rear, and in due course the adventurer was seated at a *shauri*. Kafindo was a pure Arab; and like many of the so-called emigrants from Muscat, really hailed from distant Baluchistan. His attire consisted of a robe of dark blue cloth heavily trimmed with silver, which set off his stately form to marked advantage. Behind him stalked a musician dressed in a scarlet shirt, who tapped incessantly upon a key-board strung with wires. I have already mentioned Kafindo's intelligent lecture on the course of the Lualaba; his natural courtesy found expression in a present of rice, eggs, and goat-flesh. Moreover, he promised every assistance in forwarding letters to the coast, either by way of Tanganyika or Lake Mweru. Nor did Kafindo's amiability desert him when Captain Stairs proceeded to deliver a strongly worded discourse upon the enormities of slave-raiding. This practice, said he, could not be tolerated by the King of the Belgians; more especially, as it had increased latterly to an enormous extent. Had not whole districts been devasted in Urua, so that, where there dwelt formerly a dense population, not a living soul was now to be seen. Kafindo listened in a mildly apologetic manner, admitted the unfortunate peccadillo, and undertook, with suspicious alacrity, to abandon the profession of promiscuous despoiler, and adopt instead that of legalized administrator of a prescribed territory. Strange to relate, the pledge is believed, according to the latest intelligence, to have been fairly well kept; the Baluchi continues, of course, to deal in slaves, but has relinquished his razzias for the time being. In fact the sheikh, like many of his fraternity, had been thoroughly frightened by the arrival of so many white men in his hunting-grounds; and was anxious to effect a *modus vivendi*, until he could discover the probable developments of a somewhat complex situation.

We took leave of Kafindo with much ceremony and a certain amount of respect—a sentiment hardly extended to Uturutu, another Arab whom we encountered shortly afterwards. This latter acted as Kafindo's jackal, being a person of small means, and not much strength of character. Latterly the relations between master and retainer had become strained; because, a Winchester and some cartridges having been confided to the latter's keeping, he had contrived to ruin the gun and damp the ammunition. Uturutu received us with oily servility; and was profuse in promises of friendship and material help, provided we condescended to avail ourselves of so lowly a being. There seemed, indeed, not a little of the Stiggins about Uturutu, and he belonged avowedly to the strictest sect of Islam's Pharisees. Its outward token of grace consisted in unshorn locks, which were arranged in a cheese-shaped erection not unlike the hats of Napoleon's soldiery. This mass was supposed to remain untouched by scissors for seven years, and that period seemed to be rounding to its close. Whether or no the canons of the creed also prescribed abstinence from hair-brush and soap is more than I can say; but most certainly few signs of their application appeared on the structure.

Our itinerary from Chewella may be described as follows: scattered forest varied by rivers. A high plateau lay to the south-west, but we kept pretty much in the bottom of the trough. Game abounded, and was by no means shy; hence the porters received a good meal at fairly short intervals. My readers, however, will be inclined to vote one day's shooting very much like another; so I will confine myself to the remark that the best bag was attained on the 7th of December, when Captain Bodson shot twelve antelope in one afternoon. Still there were periods when meat was not forthcoming, and then the caravan had to put up with very short commons indeed. For forty-eight hours they did not touch a bit of food; and yet on the afternoon of the second day the long line of patient wayfarers toiled into camp, and every man began, without a murmur, to build his little grass hut, cut wood, and fetch water. There was something heroic about this mute resignation to circumstances; and I fear that Tommy Atkins, under similar conditions, would hardly have displayed equal restraint. Indeed Captain Stairs remarked one evening, that, had we been dealing with British soldiers, our work would have been cut out to keep them from mutiny. Besides, empty stomachs were generally accompanied by wet skins; since the thunderstorms returned with renewed violence, accompanied by fearful gales of wind. Trenches had to be dug round the tents to prevent their being flooded; and I remember that one night, when Captain Bodson's was pitched next mine on slightly higher ground, the whole contents of his ditch came rushing into my belongings, and played complete havoc. Now boys and cook were usually accommodated under the flap of one's tent, but for the ordinary porter no such shelter was attainable; he had simply to suffer and be still.

As I have touched upon the patience displayed by the Zanzibari under supreme discomfort, the present seems a fitting occasion for describing him in love. Well, a long tragi-comedy was being enacted during this stage from Tanganyika to Bunkeya; in which the characters consisted of a porter Ali-bin-Abdullah, a woman (whose name I have forgotten), and Juma the lazy, and (on occasion), drunken askari, whose acquaintance the reader has already made. It was at a camp or two beyond Tabora that Ali appeared with the lady, whom he introduced as his wife. There was reason to believe that she was, in the eye of the law, another's; still, public opinion tolerated illicit attachments, and the pair undoubtedly entertained much mutual affection. Now at Karema Captain Stairs gave orders that no doubtful feminine should cross the lake; and as Ali's Dulcinea fell within that category, she was forbidden the boats. Nevertheless, the minx contrived to stow herself on board; and her lover's face, when she landed on the further shore, beamed with happiness unalloyed. Yet a day or two afterwards I became aware, as I sat of an evening with my face towards the lake, of a serpent in this Eden, which villain was Juma. That warrior stood about six feet three inches, and his stalwart form was decked by a prodigious quantity of brass and copper; moreover his commanding manner was backed by a persuasive tongue. He formed one of a mess, comprising also a chief and his wife, together with Mr. and Mrs. Ali. As they consumed their evening meal, Juma lost no opportunity to pay compliments to the latter dame, nor did they fall upon barren soil. Ali's suspicions were quickly on the alert, and violent quarrels ensued between him and madam, followed by equally passionate reconciliations. Still Juma continued his too-welcome addresses, with deplorable effects upon his rival's attitude towards existence. The poor fellow grew thin with anxiety; took to smoking *bhang*, a preparation of hemp, in prodigious quantities; and wandered moodily about the camp without addressing a word to his companions, though muttering constantly to himself. No love-sick schoolboy could have exhibited the tender passion with less disguise, yet the disturbers of his peace seemed absolutely callous to Ali's sufferings. The sequel was that he died of debility—I had almost written of a broken heart—at Fort Bunkeya, and Juma secured the widow. His unhallowed triumph proved, however, of brief duration; as she jilted him for a chief, and the last for a brother askari, with whom she reached Zanzibar. Thus, even in Africa, does the profound dictum of the cockney poet hold good, "You should never introduce your dona to a pal."

The most important villages passed by us, during the end of November and the beginning of December, were those of the chiefs Kifambula, Maroa, Kifuntwé, and Malagarazi. Many of these *tembés* covered a considerable area; and their inhabitants seemed an industrious set, cultivating large fields of Indian corn, *mhoga*, and *viazi*, in which stood small temporary huts to obviate a return home every evening. Everywhere we experienced a most cordial reception, and in no case did Captain Stairs encounter the smallest reluctance to accept the Congo flag. Indeed, the expedition was universally hailed as an unexpected deliverance from Msiri; and the native bands, composed almost entirely of drums, used to sound in our honour until one's head ached with the noise. On all sides appeared most visible evidences of the tyrant's sinister rule. One most curious circumstance was the extraordinary confusion of peoples and dialects collected within each palisade. The majority were Wasanga, the aboriginal tribe of the district; but mingled with them were people called Warumba, Warunda, and even Msiri's own Wanyamwesi retainers, all banded together against the common oppressor. Equally conspicuous were the number of deserted villages which had been destroyed by the king's command; even the powerful Kifambula had been compelled to shift his homestead to a point more remote from the capital. Worse still, meat was absolutely non-existent; and, as the harvest of the previous season had been carried off or destroyed by Msiri's armies, flour could only be obtained at famine prices. For a moment our hopes were raised by Malagarazi, whom we first encountered at Maroa's. He was a burly, swaggering person, a Lancashire navvy turned black as it were, and held a sub-chieftainship under Msiri, with whom he professed to be on amicable terms. Accordingly he viewed with supreme contempt such poor supplies as Maroa could produce, and exclaimed boastfully, "Yes, Maroa is a very poor man; but you come to my *tembé*. There you shall find a much goat-flesh and corn as you require." So we journeyed on with hopeful hearts, only to discover that Malagarazi's vaunted opulence resolved itself into a few handfuls of flour and some honey. However we were compelled to take the will for the deed; and Captain Stairs mended the chief's chassepot for him, whereat he seemed mightily pleased.

There could be no disguising the fact that hunger stared us in the face, and that the further we went the worse matters became. Still, the abandonment of the enterprise at its penultimate stage was scouted alike by Europeans and chiefs; on the contrary, we pressed forward with additional energy. There came, however, a week during which the men had little or nothing to eat, and many invalids had to be carried in consequence. Captain Stairs sought consolation in the fact that our stock of cloth would last for six months, or at a pinch for ten. Still, the medium of exchange would avail little if there was nothing to buy; and we had, under the most favourable circumstances, to reckon with a serious diminution of numbers from desertion and starvation.

For several days our way was through *pori*, which, owing to the general feeling of insecurity, swarmed with *ruga-ruga*. Captain Stairs thereupon ordered the men to take close order; no easy achievement, by the way, in a broken and wooded country. Nor did the officers in command of the rear-guard particularly enjoy the task of returning alone after some porters, who had managed to fall out for a nap in the bush. However, our numbers frightened the robbers, and they never offered us the smallest molestation.

The passage of the numerous rivers naturally delayed our progress; still we pressed on, and the natives gave us every assistance in the construction of bridges and so forth. By way of explanation, I may state that we crossed the Luvule at Kifambula's, and then encountered a fresh water-system in the various minor tributaries of the Luvua, as the Mpango, Luiki, and Luizi. The Luvua itself we traversed near Kifuntwé's by means of a wooden bridge, and two days afterwards struck the stream again at the point of its junction with the Lufira. This last is a river some forty feet deep, about forty-five yards wide, and with a current of two miles an hour. It has cut a channel some thirty feet below the surface of the plain, over which it describes the most capricious meanderings. We plunged down the stiff clay banks, and proceeded to put together the boats, for the crossing that day. The spot was one of wild desolation; and in thorough keeping with its general features, the actual meeting-place of the Luvua and Lufira was occupied by a deserted and overgrown *shamba*, or garden, abandoned from fear of Msiri. Not a native was to be seen, and the rank odour of damp and decaying vegetation ascended from the greasy soil. In the afternoon we saw a large waterspout bearing down on the camp; but it burst, fortunately, before reaching us, otherwise every tent would have laid even with the ground.

Soon after we left Kifuntwé's in our rear, the chief Massoudi and his escort returned from Bunkeya, and told us of a most courteous reception. Also they bore with them two letters, the first an epistle written by Mr. Crawford the missionary at Msiri's dictation, and the second the clergyman' private views as to the situation in Katanga. The official document was brevity itself, and it was written on a scrap of paper. The purport was that the king felt overjoyed at the white men's coming; he considered them his friends, and they should receive the greeting of brothers. Mr. Crawford's communication to Captain Stairs, on the other hand, contained a full account of the king's oppression, and the ruin caused thereby; indeed the general condition of the country was painted in the most sombre colours imaginable. "Well," remarked our leader, with his wonted decision, "I'll put a stop to Mr. Msiri's little games."

The passage of the Lufira was effected, thanks to Captain Stairs' orderly arrangements, in a little over four hours, the relays of men taking their places on board without a moment's delay. We then travelled through *pori*—the men foodless for thirty-six hours—until we touched the Lukulwe, which river joins the Lufira on its left bank. The tributary, like the main stream, has dug a deep bed in the surrounding plain, and soundings show its volume to be quite thirty-five feet. Moreover, it swarms with crocodiles, so that we were thankful not to have to cross, but merely to tramp along the bank except when the flood described a particularly wide curve to the east. The land appeared to be very rich, and we saw quantities of wild tomatoes. But the now too familiar ruins of villages testified to the mild and humane sway of Msiri, and in those still inhabited, the people evidently went in fear of their lives. Moreover, on the 12th of December, when we were two days from Bunkeya, the porters hired by Captain Stairs from Kifuntwé's, laid down their loads and declined to come a yard further, declaring that the king would most certainly kill them. There was nothing for it but to leave the bales in charge of the chief of the nearest village, since the pagazi were too weak to carry an additional ounce, and several sick men could only just drag themselves along.

Next day, as I was marching at the head of the cloth-carriers, some natives shouted from a neighbouring bank that a white man could be seen advancing by a cross-road. Concluding that the stranger must be one of the Wesleyan missionaries, Messrs. Crawford, Lane, and Thompson, I went down the turning to meet him. However, the first object that met my eyes was a body of strapping fellows marching along with rifles on their shoulders, and the next the Congo State flag followed by a hammock borne on a pole by four men. Who could these be? For the moment I had forgotten the existence of M. Legat, but a squat, sturdy figure soon rolled out of the netting, and introduced itself as that representative of Belgian authority. In curious contrast to their rotund leader were the eight gaunt Dahomeyans who, with sundry Wasanga acted as his escort. Nearly every man stood over six feet, and one of them had lent impressiveness to his sufficiently grim aspect by tattooing his face in the most elaborate manner. With some blunt instrument he had dug a series of small pits, arranged in parallel lines, all over his forehead and cheeks, forcing the flesh outwards so that it formed a sort of lip.

As we walked along our line towards Captain Stairs, M. Legat talked freely of the general situation. He drew a lurid picture of Msiri's cruelties, and the consequent famine, civil war, and general disorder. This state of affairs, he added, could not possibly continue; even if we did not intervene, the insurgents were eventually bound to get the upper hand, and the most merciful course would be to put as speedy a check to the bloodshed as possible. In his opinion, Msiri would gladly evacuate the country in favour of the Wasanga, if he could be certain of finding a resting-place on the further side of Lake Mweru. As for the missionaries, M. Legat explained that Mr. Arnot, the original founder of the station about a mile to the south-west of Bunkeya had not yet arrived, as he was unable to get together a caravan at Benguela. Messrs. Crawford, Lane, and Thompson had been compelled by the tyrant's insolence and caprice to leave the capital and build a station on the Lifoi some twenty-four miles away, so as to escape his daily contumely, and obtain the protection of the Belgian fort. The lieutenant related, with some humour, the supreme contempt with which Msiri had received a present of silver-plate and cloth sent by some good Christians from Glasgow. The metal was consigned to his back kitchen; and the fabric defined as good enough for his slaves, but not for his wives. M. Legat also chuckled over his own "score" off a half-caste trader from Angola. It appeared that the latter arrived at Bunkeya with the Portuguese flag hoisted. Whereupon Belgian bile was stirred; and the old man was given the alternatives of boxing the flag, or expulsion from the country. After a considerable amount of bluster, he surrendered his pretensions, and the obnoxious standard disappeared.

As for the other Belgian expeditions, Lieutenant Legat could give us little positive information. No news of Captain Bia's approach had arrived, accordingly there was no possibility of calculating the length of our stay in Katanga. Also nothing had been heard of M. Delcommune since he had passed southwards from Bunkeya. M. Legat gave us a graphic description of his compatriot's difficulties on the Lualaba, and declared that he intended, as the result of his experiences, to return by the Lomami and Congo. His present whereabouts, however, and his success or failure in discovering gold were equally unknown.

On quitting M. Legat we descended a small range of hills; and on the following day, after a most tiresome march across a shadeless, waterless plain, flanked on either side by mountain peaks the camp was pitched late in the afternoon about a mile from the capital.

Chapter X

Msiri

Rapidity of our progress—Dearness of provisions—Approach of the *masika*—Msiri's career—His arrival in Katanga—Accession to the throne—Trade opened with the West Coast—Coimbra and Maria—Enlargement of Msiri's boundaries—His espionage and oppression—The civil war—Msiri's dealings with the white men—The missionaries—Msiri's personal appearance.

THUS the 14th of December, 1891, found the expedition at its destination, Bunkeya the capital of Msiri, the King of Katangaland. Our journey from Bagamoyo on the east coast had taken five months and ten days, during which time we had made one hundred and twenty marches, consisting, on an average, of about eight miles apiece. This we flattered ourselves to be a "record" in African travel, and in other respects the caravan had been particularly fortunate. Not a single load had been lost, and but five rifles were missing out of the two hundred. The fact is that Captain Stairs commanded an exceptionally fine body of men, and one very different from the riff-raff of the bazaars which accompanied Commander Cameron on his famous walk across Africa. Yet admirable though the discipline and endurance of our rank and file had been, I could see that the daily exertion had told upon them. The features of the white men looked particularly pinched and drawn; and even the Zanzibaris were sadly changed from the sleek and corpulent individuals whose acquaintance we had made in June. Clearly the essentials were a long rest and good feeding; but the former condition was of doubtful attainment, and the latter impossible.

I have already mentioned the dismal intelligence, and still more lamentable evidence, we had obtained along the road of the famine caused by Msiri's cruelties and the consequent civil war. Well, the signs of desolation increased a hundred-fold during the last stages of our approach to Bunkeya. Upon the face of the vast plain not a cow was to be seen, only a few sheep and goats pasturing at long intervals.

Still more significant were the ruins of villages whose inhabitants had fled from Msiri's exactions of produce, and, worse still, his demand for their wives and daughters. For years the stream of emigration had been flowing, with little intermission, until but a poor remnant remained, Heart-broken by the tyrant's oppressions, these unhappy creatures had ceased to cultivate the fields no corn was procurable, only a little *matamah*. This sold at exorbitant prices; thus about half a peck cost four "hands" of cloth, and a fowl could not be procured for less than three. We heard that the food in Bunkeya would only last for seven or eight days, on half rations. Already there came complaints from the porters that they only received a quarter of their usual allowance; and I know that my larder would have been woefully empty, had it not been for the antelope I had shot. Evidently our position was none of the most encouraging so far as commissariat was concerned.

We were also threatened by another source of sickness and discomfort, namely, the approach of the constant winter rains, which had been heralded by the thunderstorms I have described. The evening after we arrived a downpour began, and continued nearly through the night. On the 18th a terrific hurricane arose after dark; which I thought would have carried away my tent, though fortunately the tackle held. These were nature's warnings that we should do well to get our men hutted without further delay. But the question was easier asked than answered—will Msiri consent to the building of a fort at the gates of his capital, or shall we have to fight him for the privilege?

The political situation can hardly be understood without a brief description of Msiri's career, which possesses besides a certain romantic interest not unlike that associated with the names of the great Italian condottieri. He came from Garenganze, a province of distant Unyanyembe, where his father Kalassa held a minor chieftainship under the mighty Mirambo. Now this Kalassa was a man of great enterprise, particularly as a trader in copper; and he made frequent journeys across the water into the land of the Wasanga—for so, as I have already mentioned, the original inhabitants of this region are called. He soon wormed himself into the confidence of the old chief of the district, and, established what a trade newspaper would call a "most lucrative connection". About thirty years ago Kalassa was prevented from some cause from paying one of these annual visits;

accordingly, his son Msiri went in his stead. With a keen eye to business, the youth took with him no less than four guns, a weapon then absolutely unknown in Central Africa. The precaution proved distinctly valuable, since, on his arrival, he discovered the Wasanga at war with Balunda, a tribe hailing from the north. Msiri promptly offered his services to his father's friend; and the enemy, at the first discharge of the miracle-working machines, fled helter-skelter. The aged chief was naturally overwhelmed with gratitude; he made large presents of ivory to the young man, and pressed him to return ere many months had passed. Msiri responded to the invitation with remarkable readiness, nor did he come back alone. He appeared at the head of a large caravan of wives, children, and Wanyamwesi followers, and announced that he would never again desert his venerable benefactor. The latter's reply is unrecorded by history; but he appears to have submitted to the inevitable, to have passed the remainder of his days in honourable captivity, and, at his death, to have left the succession to Msiri. Thus this clear-headed adventurer rose to be king of the Wasanga, and he promptly secured his position by the massacre of all opponents, actual or potential.

The first step taken by the new potentate stamps him as a born conqueror of men. He saw that whoso had guns and powder, held Central Africa in the hollow of his hand. Now, from his boyhood, ho had heard of the great sheet of water to the east, whence the white merchants came with supplies of these indispensable commodities. But in his present position they were obviously liable to be intercepted by the kings, his rivals; and thus independence could never be achieved. Accordingly he proceeded to send his nephew Molenga at the head of an exploring expedition, to discover the other vast ocean that was said to lie far away in the west. Molenga went on his way; and as he journeyed, came across various Portuguese traders from the province of Angola upon the Atlantic seaboard. To them he related his story, how a powerful chief many marches distant had much ivory to barter for weapons of war. The half-caste mentioned in the last chapter, Coimbra by name—though the natives called him Houja—promptly took the hint, and conveyed several caravans of powder, rifles, and shot to Msiri's capital. He became highly esteemed by Msiri, and by way of cementing the acquaintance gave the king his sister Maria in wedlock. We saw this man on several occasions; and, despite his fracas with M. Legat, he appeared remarkably intelligent, besides being free from complicity in his brother-in-law's cruelties. Maria lived in a village of her own not far from Bunkeya, and it was not long before we made her acquaintance also. She was a mulatto woman about forty-five years of age, and I can hardly risk a fair reputation for veracity by calling her handsome. They were both far superior to the Swahili scoundrel who acted as Maria's prime minister.

Thanks to his statesman-like acquisition of weapons of precision, Msiri soon became master of an extensive empire. He defied the former suzerain of the Wasanga, the powerful chief Kasembé who lived on Lake Mweru; and' that sovereign was compelled to withdraw discomfited from an attempt to chastise the rebellious upstart. He annexed the Luba country to the west, and the Lunda territory to the north. During those years of perpetual campaigns he was careful to keep up the fighting strength of his army by constant drafts of his Wanyamwesi countrymen; and his favourite wife, Chitompa, proved an expert tactician, who never returned without a goodly supply of skulls. To cut short Msiri's annals of conquest, I may say that the boundaries of his kingdom extended to the Lualaba on the east, and the Kasai on the west; on the north to Lake Upamba, and on the south to the mountains dividing the Zambesi system from that of the Congo. All this country was under his immediate rule, and he exacted tribute from a district at least as large again.

From Msiri, the warrior, it is impossible to withhold admiration; Msiri, the administrator, developed into a far less praiseworthy personage. Certain instincts of government he undoubtedly possessed; for instance, he encouraged the arrival of traders from all parts of Africa. From Zanzibar, from Uganda, from the Zambesi, from Angola, and from the Congo basin, came merchants who exchanged ammunition and cloth for ivory, copper, and slaves. The Arabs also succeeded in foisting upon Msiri a wonderful collection of musical-boxes, concertinas, American clocks, a policeman's uniform, and all kinds of firearms, some good and others indifferent. This curious acquisitiveness, however, was by no means peculiar to Msiri among African monarchs; and real genius for rule was displayed in his division of the country among a number of minor chiefs, with a set of officials under them. But there the wisdom of his policy ended; for his methods of government embraced every kind of espionage and oppression. The whole country was honeycombed by spies and informers, and the overseers were compelled to surrender their wives and daughters as securities for good behaviour

Thus at Bunkeya he collected an enormous harem of women whose children were styled his sons, though they often bore him no blood relationship whatever. He entertained the true tyrant's love of servility; even his own brother Chikako had to kiss the dust before him, only to be addressed by "son of a dog," and other opprobrious terms.

His extortions were manifold; thus every tusk of ivory had to be brought to the capital, and, if an official was suspected of concealing the precious material, woe betide him. In the dead of night the royal soldiers would surround the village; it would be reduced to ashes, and the people sold into slavery. The offender was lucky if he escaped with instant death, for Msiri delighted in diabolical refinements of cruelty. Quite minor crimes were punished by the lopping of a hand or the docking of an ear; in fact, Msiri practised mutilation almost as extensively as Kasongo, that Waruan barbarian whom Commander Cameron has depicted. Those who incurred a larger share of the royal displeasure were buried in the earth up to the neck and then left to starve, or shut into a hut with hungry village dogs to be eaten alive. When Captain Stairs went up to Bunkeya, the row of stakes surmounted by human heads, that encircled the village, gave him considerable insight into Msiri's character and methods of administration.

No doubt the government of a congeries of tribes, differing alike in dialect and disposition, presented problems by no means easy of solution. Msiri's rule has found its apologists; and very likely at the outset, he may have exercised no more than a reasonable amount of severity. It may be that his disposition degenerated through the approach of crabbed old age, and the consciousness that, with all his labours, he had been unable to found a stable dynasty. At any rate his barbarities became unendurable, and the Wasanga, after years of bondage and suffering, rose in revolt. They allied themselves with the Balunda, the Baramba, and other little tribes; and the confederacy, from its highland fastnesses, waged a guerrilla warfare against the common oppressor. Even the Wanyamwesi legionaries, wearied of Msiri's caprice, went over to the enemy, who received them with open arms. On our march, as I have already said, we passed more than one village of various nationalities, living in harmony together under a chief who as often as not was a Wanyamwesi; such was the confusion of peoples produced by Msiri's grinding despotism. For more than nine months before our arrival the desultory struggle had been in progress, without any marked advantage to either side. Still the anti-Msiri league gradually made headway; the king's authority was practically confined within a radius of fourteen miles from the capital, and he could depend on none except his immediate following. So desperate had his position become, that, as M. Legat had surmised, he actually contemplated retiring from Katangaland, and building a village in British territory on the further side of Lake Mweru; but was deterred by the difficulty of obtaining a sufficient number of boats.

Unfortunately too, his intellect, now in its dotage, was unable to grapple with the complications produced by the presence of white men representing conflicting interests. I have already given a brief outline of the expedition of Mr. Sharpe on behalf of the British South African Company, and of MM. le Marinel and Delcommune, as representatives of the king of the Belgians. Of these various embassies that of M. le Marinel had narrowly missed its aim; and his lieutenant, M. Legat, had undoubtedly obtained a marked ascendancy over the Wanyamwesi potentate, considering the handful of men at his disposal. Still, no one had been able to extract from Msiri an act of submission, or to persuade him to hoist either the British or the Belgian flag. With senile cunning he evidently proposed to foment jealousies between white and white, and so to preserve his independence by a judicious source of trimming.

Such, with its various bearings, was the situation with which Captain Stairs had to deal. I should also remind the reader that the rumoured approach of the South Africa Company's expedition, under Mr. Joseph Thomson, caused a prompt solution of our difficulties with Msiri to be a matter of urgent necessity. On the other hand, we were hampered by the presence in Katangaland of the three English Missionaries, Messrs. Crawford, Lane, and Thompson who had latterly taken the places of Messrs. Arnot, Faulkner, and Swan, though the author of *Garenganze* was about to return. These worthy men had endured for several years the utmost contumely at the hands of Msiri. He used to call them his "white slaves", insult them before the public, and despoil them of their goods. The result of the royal displeasure was that, after six years' work, the mission had not secured a single convert, and, as M. Legat had informed us, was finally compelled to leave the capital, and build a station on the Lifoi, near the Belgian fort. Even so their position was none of the most secure; and Captain Stairs felt that if it came to blows with Msiri, the latter might wreak his vengeance upon our defenceless fellow-countrymen. He wished, therefore, to get them safely out of Katangaland before taking decisive action.

I fear that my description of Msiri's character can hardly be considered complimentary. On the other hand, I am bound to say that his appearance was impressive, and his demeanour thoroughly regal. Though he had begun to stoop somewhat with age, he stood fully six feet high, and must have weighed, as I afterwards had occasion to know, some fourteen stone. He had good features, an aquiline nose, and a well-shaped head. His hair swept his shoulders, and he wore a short beard which had turned quite white. There was a sphinx- like impenetrability about his expression, yet his large gestures gave emphasis and variety to his conversation. In his prime, Msiri must have looked the ideal of a warrior-king; he was by no means contemptible in his decline. As for his attire, it consisted of a greasy handkerchief by way of head-dross, a silk cloak covered with gold lace, a pair of old trousers, and huge jack-boots, in which he shuffled along, none too comfortably.

CHAPTER XI

THE FIGHT

Three days' delay—Captain Stairs' first palaver with Msiri—The second *shauri*—The flag hoisted—Msiri's chicanery—His flight to Munema—Captain Bodson sent to take him prisoner—News from the front—The appearance of Munema—Captain Bodson's entry into the town—The Marquis to the rescue— Our men loot the village—Hamadi's narrative—I proceed to the relief—Lukuku and Chikako—Through the streets of Munema—The scene in the central square—Order restored— We evacuate the village—Msiri's body—Death of Captain Bodson—His burial—Captain Stairs' official report.

THE three days' delay, demanded by negro etiquette before Captain Stairs' interview with the king, passed wearily enough. We white men were longing for action, and had to put up with idleness upon short commons. To vary the monotony of the situation I was visited by a sharp stroke of fever, which rendered the task of attending the sick men extremely irksome. During the interval of suspense we saw something of M. Legat, a most capable man; and the missionaries paid us several visits. They seemed much oppressed by the hopelessness of their position; and we could not help thinking that a profound mistake was committed, when they were despatched into this barbarous country hundreds of miles from a European post. The natives strolled into the camp from time to time, and appeared well-nourished, considering the famine. The women had a fair allowance of good looks, and wore spiral circlets round the neck and arms; but their morals were to seek. Curiously enough they did not eat goat-flesh or fowls; but whether from religious causes, or as a sign of their inferiority to the males, we were unable to discover.

On the17th, Captain Stairs went with an escort to Bunkeya, and had a long palaver with Msiri. We awaited the upshot with some anxiety; and our disappointment was extreme when we learnt, on his return, that no understanding had been effected. It appeared that he had been received by the king with the greatest cordiality, in the hope that we should co-operate in driving M. Legat from the country. Captain Stairs affected to entertain the idea, and promised in addition to help in reducing the Wasanga and their allies. Still Msiri declined to make "blood brotherhood", or to hoist the Belgian flag, while Stairs as steadily refused to supply him with powder. Finally, the conversation took a somewhat acrimonious turn. Msiri was given plainly to understand that his monstrous cruelties could no longer be tolerated, he was also warned that the missionaries must not be molested. Msiri professed to be extremely loth to let them go, and sent another message to that effect on the following day. He was informed in reply that the white men, Stairs and Legat, were responsible for their security; and that any one who tried to detain them, would be shot without ceremony.

Thus affairs seemed to have reached a deadlock. Either Msiri was unable to make up his mind to a definite line of action; or he was attempting to gain time, so as to collect his scattered forces, and then fall upon the expedition. But in Captain Stairs he encountered an opponent with whom procrastination did not pay. A second *shauri* was arranged for the 19th; and in the afternoon our leader, accompanied by the Marquis de Bonchamps and thirty askaris, went up to Bunkeya, taking with him the Congo State flag. He told Captain Bodson to keep a sharp look-out, and to be ready to give assistance in case of emergency. For several hours Bodson and I stood on an ant-heap with our field-glasses turned towards Bunkeya. About 5 p.m. we saw Stairs, Bonchamps, and the soldiers issue from the town, climb the steep hill at the back, and plant a pole upon which speedily floated the blue flag with its yellow star. We naturally thought that all difficulties were at an end, and prepared to receive our companions with hearty congratulations. As they drew near the camp, however, there was a certain look of disappointment in their faces, and we learnt that Msiri had a second time, failed to come to a decision.

For close upon four hours Captain Stairs plied argument upon argument to induce him to accept the Belgian flag. At first the king would have no flag at all; then he was willing to receive the *Ingreza* (English) flag, but not that of the Free State. He disavowed the letter of submission secured by M. le Marinel, and declared that not only would he refuse to sign such document himself, but that any of his subjects who did so would be treated as enemies and rebels.

Finally he professed his readiness to accept the Belgian symbol of sovereignty on the morrow, when his brother Chikako should exchange blood with Captain Stairs in token of perpetual friendship. "No," was the answer, "I shall make blood brotherhood to-day, and with you; and then I shall hoist the flag." After further protestation Msiri rose to re-enter his compound; upon which Captain Stairs said, "Very well; since we have come to this, I shall hoist the flag whether you desire it or not." He had taken the stake from Msiri's own palisade, and no opposition had been offered, either in the streets of Bunkeya, or during the ascent of the hill.

Our rest was disturbed that night, as we fully expected that Msiri, having collected his warriors, would attack the camp, in which case it would have gone hard with us. The morning dawned, however, without mishap, when Stairs sent no less than four messages to Msiri to the effect that he was ready to make blood brotherhood. The answer came back each time that his majesty slept; and as the day wore on, Stairs determined to put an end to the poor comedy by taking Msiri prisoner. Just as Bodson and the Marquis were about to start on the hazardous enterprise (9 a.m.), we learnt that Msiri had fled from Bunkeya by night, and taken himself to Munema, a village about three miles off. We advanced, therefore, to Maria's village and took up a strong position. Legat and ten of his Dahomeyan soldiers joined us; and we sent an escort to the missionaries on the Lifoi to conduct them to the Free State fort without delay, with a message that war was inevitable.

At eleven o'clock, Captain Bodson and the Marquis de Bonchamps, with a hundred and fifteen rifles and a corporal of Legat's for guide, were again dispatched to arrest Msiri. The detachment bore a fairly martial appearance; but I did not envy their undertaking, as the men had never faced a fusillade and their conduct on more than one occasion during the march had cast a certain doubt upon their valour. They reached Munema, nearly two miles off, about midday, and half an hour afterwards heavy firing began. Through my glass I could see our askaris peppering the west front of the village, and it was clear that Msiri had shown his teeth. Stairs being engaged in reconnoitring about a quarter of a mile off, I made dispositions to protect our camp, and succeeded in getting the men into fair order. the circuit, however, was so large that it would have taken at least eight hundred men to guard it properly, and I could not help feeling that we lay at the mercy of a determined enemy. At that moment the chief, Khamis Ngozi, came rushing back from Munema with a handful of askari. As soon as they could speak, I learned that Captain Bodson and two Zanzibaris were wounded, and everything in confusion.

It was not until many hours afterwards that we were able to piece together the sequence of that eventful morning. Captain Bodson and the Marquis de Bonchamps, as I have already related, arrived at the outskirts of Munema shortly after twelve o'clock; and the more they examined the place, the less did they like its appearance. The village consisted of a collection of some hundred huts, scattered over a considerable space. Its defences comprised the usual boma of thick paling; while round each house stood smaller bulwarks, formed of sticks or thick hedges of euphorbia. Thus there was a first and a second line of resistance; while the spaces between the huts, being extremely narrow, formed, as it were, a network of blind alleys, in which the attacking force would fight under great disadvantages. The natives seemed to be little disconcerted by the presence of Captain Bodson's contingent; and from time to time a fighting man, armed, as a rule, with a rifle, showed himself from behind the enclosures.

Captain Bodson drew up his little band in line, with its back to the hills and facing the village. After a quarter of an hour a chief came forward, and asked what the white men wished. The answer was that they desired to see and talk with Msiri; at the same time assurance was given that the king alone was the object of the visit, and that no harm should happen to the inhabitants. "Good," returned the chief, "then follow me." In spite of Bonchamps' remonstrances, Bodson—than whom no braver man has ever penetrated into the Dark Continent—determined to risk the adventure. He took with him but ten men and two chiefs, including, of course, the excellent Hamadi; leaving the Marquis with instructions to attack directly the signal was given—two shots from his revolver.

The period of suspense was not long. In less than ten minutes crack went the pistol, and the louder report of several rifles followed. M. de Bonchamps promptly advanced, and was received by a fairly steady fire. His men wavered; but the Marquis rallied them in the most resolute manner, and the whole force dashed past the boma and through the little streets. As they drew near the central square, the sight of several natives in full flight encouraged their hopes; but, when the goal was reached, these sanguine expectations proved sadly illusory. Before the king's hut lay poor Bodson, badly wounded in the abdomen. Near him was stretched Msiri, hit in several places. Farther off lay another Wanyamwesi, one of the king's relatives. In a corner were an askari and the gallant Hamadi, the former with both legs broken, and the other with a ball in his ankle.

When the Marquis put in his timely appearance, the skirmish was still in progress; but the mere sight of his hundred or so of askaris drove the enemy to rout. A flying foe and a village to sack form inducements that the Zanzibari temperament cannot resist. Regardless of the fact that, if Msiri's followers returned, the position, under the best of circumstances, would be barely tenable, they scattered in all directions, some pillaging the huts, and others taking snap shots at the unfortunate fugitives, as they dodged like rabbits in and out of the alleys. Unable to leave Captain Bodson, who was evidently in great pain, M. de Bonchamps did his best to keep a handful of men together in the central square. Hamadi's subsequent account of the tragedy ran something as follows:—

"We followed the Wanyamwesi chief, and he took us to the central square. There sat Msiri before his house, with two of his wives, and some three hundred warriors, nearly all armed with guns. Their appearance was most hostile, and I saw that our danger was great. Nevertheless the little chief [Captain Bodson] advanced and spoke to Msiri. 'O king,' said he, 'arise and follow me. I will lead you to the camp of the great white chief [Captain Stairs], and no evil shall happen to your person.' But Msiri seemed very angry, and answered not a word, but ground his teeth with wrath. Suddenly he arose and laid his hand upon the sword, the gift of the great chief. He meant to kill the Captain, but the latter drew his revolver and fired— I think thrice. I also shot twice at the king, and he fell. At that moment, a puff of smoke appeared at the corner of the verandah, and I could see a man lying with his rifle pointed towards the little chief. The latter sank by my side with a groan; and the Dahomeyan corporal, who acted as our guide, shot the captain's assailant as he turned to run away. Then the firing became general; I was wounded in the ankle, and lay in great pain until our askaris appeared. And that is all that Hamadi-bin-Malum knows."

Such was the deplorable situation of which I was informed, in epitome, by the chief Khamis Ngozi. Fortunately Captain Stairs had by this time returned to Maria's, and he ordered me to proceed at once to the relief. Taking with me twenty men, I started for Munema at the double. We had to pass under a hill, upon which appeared Chikako and Lukuku, the king's brothers, his son Makanda Vanta, and two or three hundred Wanyamwesi, all brandishing their rifles and evidently meaning mischief. I afterwards learnt that their original intention had been to attack us in Maria's village; but, alarmed by the state of affairs in Munema, they proposed the safer manoeuvre of cutting off Captain Bodson's retreat. They saluted us with a hot, but ill-directed fire; and on we went, without any losses.

Arrived outside the village, I found a small body of askaris, who, I afterwards discovered, had been stationed there by M. de Bonchamps to prevent the enemy from re-entering the boma. They shouted to us, "Don't go on; there are men in ambush ahead." My fellows promptly turned back, with the exception of two porters, Ismalia and Mirabo Ngumba, of whom the latter had served in the Emin Relief Expedition as bearer of a portion of the Maxim gun. We passed the ambush—a loopholed boma—without mishap; and then, turning sharp to the right, I found myself in a perfect maze of huts, surrounded by the stiff palisades that I have already described. The ping of several bullets against the woodwork brought me to my bearings; and, looking round, I saw a group of natives, some of whom were firing at us. I returned the compliment, and bowled over several of them with my Winchester. Then a few askaris came to my assistance, and began letting off their guns in all directions, yelling the while like fiends. I promptly knelt down, and remained in that attitude for several minutes, and so escaped being shot in the back. At last I got the men into line, and we advanced in some semblance of order, though they shouted with true Zanzibari vigour of lung, and fired wildly at the flying natives. My bullies, indeed, displayed astonishing valour, when they discovered that the enemy invariably ran. We charged through an apparently endless labyrinth of streets, until by good luck, Charles, one of the porters, met us, and pointed out the way to the centre of the village. As we drew near, I heard a hullabaloo that could proceed only from Zanzibari throats. I rushed in quickly, so as to show myself before our braves had time to fire.

The place was a perfect pandemonium. Before his house lay Msiri on his back, stone dead. He had three bullet wounds, two from Bodson and one from Hamadi. The Captain seemed *in extremis*, while the unfortunate askari and Hamadi were writhing and groaning with pain. Their outcries, however, were drowned by the roarings of our illustrious soldiery. The Marquis de Bonchamps was making strenuous efforts to restore discipline; but the men had lost all sense of obedience in the excitement of the loot. One had seized a shrieking woman, another was struggling with a refractory goat. Here a soldier was hunting down a fowl, and there a porter was walking off with a load of furniture. It was no time for mild measures, as the enemy might return in force at any moment. So I took up a thick stake and commenced laying about me to the right and left. Eventually, we made the men sit down, and placed chiefs over them with instructions to fire in case of a fresh outbreak. Then we hastily made litters for the two wounded Zanzibari, placed Captain Bodson in a hammock I had brought for the purpose, and evacuated Munema with all speed. We also bore off the body of Msiri, so that his sons could not return, bury it by stealth, and then give out that the great king was alive and in hiding. Thereby they would have been able to continue the war against the Wasanga, and our plans for the settlement of the country would have been utterly foiled.

The journey to the camp was accomplished without mishap, as Chikako and Lukuku left us severely alone. The Marquis led the way through the gate on the west side of the village, escorting Captain Bodson and the other wounded men. I followed with eight men who bore the corpse of Msiri. The heat was terrific, the fellows exhausted by the day's exertions, the body of prodigious weight. Frequent halts were necessary, sometimes the burden descended to its mother-earth with a crash. And all the while I expected that the Wanyamwesi would descend upon us, and rescue their sovereign's remains. In the midst of these predicaments I happened to glance at the dead man's face. It seemed to wear a mocking smile which, somehow, was not easily forgotten.

When we got into camp I found that poor Bodson was sinking fast. His destroyer, whom we afterwards discovered to have been a favourite slave of Msiri's, had wounded him in a vital spot, and no human art could have availed. After enduring with unflagging constancy some terrible suffering, he breathed his last at eight in the evening. A few moments before, he whispered, "Doctor, I don't mind dying, now that I have killed Msiri." To Captain Stairs he delivered the following message for his fellow-countrymen. "Thank God, my death will not be in vain. I have delivered Africa from one of her most detestable tyrants."

Next day we buried the body hard by the camp, having dug the grave deep so that the natives could not rifle its contents. At half-past eleven the melancholy procession was formed. Four chiefs bore the litter, followed by eleven askaris, all armed to the teeth. We had to make quick work from fear of the enemy. The remains were reverently deposited in the trench, the earth filled hi, and then Robinson handed the Marquis a small wooden cross to place at his dead comrade's head. And there in a strange land, we left this illustrious member of the company of travellers in Africa.

"This unhappy death," wrote Captain Stairs in his official report, "has deprived the expedition of a capable and energetic official, of a faithful man, full of zeal for the accomplishment of his duty, and always ready to carry out every instruction. I had become his friend, and I can appreciate his thorough fitness for his undertaking, and his capacities for work in Africa. His abilities certainly marked him out as one destined to gain a high position in the affairs of the Congo, had not death cut off his career in this unfortunate fashion."[*]

---

[*] From Captain Stairs' official report, as published in *Le Mouvement Géographie*, of July 26th, 1892.

CHAPTER XII

FORT BUNKEYA

We leave Maria's—Illness of M. de Bonchamps—Lazy sentinels—The burial of Msiri—The succession question—Makanda Vanta recognized—Coimbra departs—The flag hoisted at Makanda Vanta's—Lukuku's Contumacy—Chikako comes in—Settlement of the valley—Fort Bunkeya—The towers—The inner space—A conflagration—Christmas Day—A proposed expedition to Mweru—Imminence of famine—Reports of white men on the Luapula—The story disproved—Illness of Captain Stairs—I am left alone—The pangs of hunger—A reminiscence of the Strand—My second-self—Fidelity of the chiefs—Mortality amongst the men—The cemetery—Our relations with the natives—A mutiny suppressed—Robbery of arms—Settlement of Katanga—Mutwila's gold-mine—Garden parties—The Zanzibari's merits and demerits—Food at last—Captain Stairs' continued illness—No news of Delcommune—Arrival of Captain Bia—His adventures.

AFTER burying poor Captain Bodson, we quitted Maria's, and proceed to a large deserted village on some rising ground about two miles to the south of Bunkeya, which Captain Stairs' professional eye had selected for the site of the projected fort. Its strategic advantages were considerable, as no cover grew upon the slopes, nor could the natives command the position from any superior height. There was also, of course, plenty of water during the *masika*, though in the dry season it would have to be fetched from wells eight hundred yards away. But in the construction of the station we were greatly hampered by the loss of Captain Bodson; more especially as the Marquis de Bonchamps, who seemed stunned by his friend's death, took to his bed a day or two afterwards with a bad attack of fever. Robinson very speedily followed his example; so that the commander and myself were the only two white men fit for duty. And hard work it was, more especially as, until our defences neared completion, the Wasanga could have surprised the camp in the darkness, seized the loads and "smashed up" the expedition. Accordingly we had to stand on the alert by night as well as by day, and to visit the sentries at least three times in the small hours. As the Marquis did not recover, Captain Stairs and I had to take the night-watches alternately; so that little sleep was obtainable for half the week—while rest in the daytime was rendered impossible by the flies.

It must be confessed that the occupation of going the rounds by no means tended to an evenness of temper. During the first week or so one invariably found the askaris either asleep, or else laughing and chattering without the slightest attempt to keep a look-out. So annoyed was I, that, one night, on catching a fellow snoring, I brought him to his waking senses by a smart blow across the back with his rifle. Thereupon the weapon promptly broke in two—an accident which showed that "company's" guns at nine shillings apiece, were hardly the sort of tools with which a sensible man would care to defend his life. Moreover, several of the soldiers complained that in the fight at Munema their rifles would not act; wherefore the condition of our armament by no means made for confidence. The conduct of the sentinels, however, decidedly improved, as they became used to the work, and imbued with some slight sense of discipline.

Fortunately the inhabitants of the valley were possessed by no desire to avenge Msiri's death. On the morrow of the fight a messenger appeared in camp with a request that the body might be surrendered; and, Captain Stairs having given his consent, Lukuku, Chikako, and Makanda Vanta appeared with a numerous train of drummers and—if I may venture upon a bull—most vocal mutes Amidst a hideous din of tom-toms and human howling the great king's corpse was borne across the plain to the royal burial-ground, and interred with much ring of guns and drinking of pombé. But the wake over, Msiri's relatives recovered their spirits with surprising rapidity; indeed a certain feeling that he was best underground appeared to prevail. At any rate the immediate interest of the Succession question soon absorbed their somewhat circumscribed intelligences.

On the 23rd of December a deputation, consisting of Chikako and Makanda Vanta, with the support of Coimbra the Portuguese half-caste and Maria, arrived to discuss the knotty point. Captain Stairs promptly held a *shauri*, and the tongues wagged incessantly for many hours, Maria, who bore her widowhood with curious cheerfulness, taking a most prominent part in the palaver. Now he had already determined the lines upon which the settlement had best be effected, and these conditions he proposed to enforce, if necessary by armed demonstration. Makanda Vanta was to be recognized as Msiri's heir, and made ruler of the fourteen square miles upon which Bunkeya stands; while to his uncles, Chikako and Lukuku, were to be assigned small sub-chieftainships comprising their respective villages and the appurtenant fields. The remainder of the Katanga country was to be handed over to the Wasanga chiefs, who were to be restored, so far as the lapse of time would permit, to the position held by themselves or their ancestors, before the advent of the Wanyamwesi conqueror. In short, Captain Stairs aimed at the establishment of a petty balance of power, upon which the memory of the universal oppressor would act as conservative influence.

Directly the scheme was broached, signs of consternation appeared on every countenance. Hands were uplifted, woolly heads set in violent commotion, and any arrangement comprising less than the assignment of the whole of Katanga scouted as absolutely unacceptable. Captain Stairs explained with some decision that no departure from the plan could be countenanced and then, knowing his company, left the deputation to talk. After every argument geographical, genealogical, chronological, and irrelevant had been exhausted three or four times over, the general conclusion was that the great white chief's commands should be obeyed. Indeed the Makanda Vanta interest, as represented by himself, made little attempt to conceal its satisfaction; the treaty was signed, and arrangements made for the hoisting of the Belgian flag on the 30th.

During the next few days Captain Stairs was condemned to numerous *shauris* with Maria and Coimbra. The brother and sister evidently regarded themselves most agreeable conversationalists, and thought that the Englishman could have no better occupation than to talk about the weather. Besides they desired some assistance in coming to a decision as to their future course of action. The trader felt his occupation gone, and desired to return to Portuguese territory. The lady, however, having tasted the delights of sovereignty, felt sorely loth to relinquish them. Finally, after an animated family quarrel, Coimbra started for the coast alone with the intention of returning for Maria in the course of the summer. The two took their leave with much ceremony, and went chattering off to the widow's *tembé*.

On the appointed day I started with six askaris to hoist the flag in Makanda Vanta's village. By Captain Stairs' directions, we took a pole twenty feet long, which had to be so planted that it could not be removed except by violence. The job proved by no means easy, as within a few feet of the surface we came upon the rock, at which the men hammered and dug for the best part of three hours. Finally the staff was erected, the earth beaten down about it, and my initials with the date carved just below the flag. Captain Stairs grew alarmed at the delay, and sent a messenger to discover why we were absent from camp so long. The envoy, however, lighted upon a most peaceful scene; as Makanda Vanta and myself were seated side by side, the newly installed potentate busily engaged in mending a German concertina, upon which he played with some skill. He seemed indeed a well-disposed youth, about twenty-six years of age, straightforward and by no means deficient in common sense. His sonship to Msiri was that of adoption merely, and I should say that he must have been a full-blooded Wasanga, though he had assumed, of course, the Wanyamwesi tribal marks. The natives showed every confidence in his rule, as they had already established themselves in large numbers round his hut; so that corner-stone of the Katanga hegemony seemed to be well and truly laid.

His uncles, Lukuku and Chikako, however, were less amenable to reason. Disappointed with their portions, they failed to appear on the 27th, when they should have signed their treaties; nor did they condescend to apologize for their contumacy. The former, however, was brought to a humbler frame of mind by Tuwilla, a Wasanga chieftain, who, on hearing of Msiri's death, promptly proceeded to make a declaration of war, which overture Lukuku declined with thanks. Thereupon he sent a most effusive message to Captain Stairs. Would the great white chief declare his intentions towards his slave, who knew not whether to feel secure of protection, or as one condemned to death? Simultaneously, Tuwilla despatched ambassadors with an admirably carved fetish; namely, a stool, fashioned into the shape of a woman keeling, with a child at one of her breasts. However, the quarrel between the two being composed,

Lukuku resorted to his former delays and evasions. So affairs drifted for over a month; until, by Captain Stairs' orders, I repaired to his village with fifty men, and told him that unless the treaty was signed forthwith, he should share the fate of Msiri. Chikako had already come to terms; and, on the 26th of January, Lukuku came into the fort and made formal act of submission.

The contrast between the two *shauris* was extremely curious. Lukuku, a small wizened old man, evidently considered his neck none too secure on his shoulders; and, after affixing his mark to the paper, he hurried away at a sharp trot. Chikako on the contrary, who was a strongly built barbarian, in the prime of life, conversed at his ease on the topics of the day. At first he attempted to carry matters with a high hand: "I must have that village, and that, and that." When, however, it was explained that for him remained only the choice of Hobson, he bowed to the decree of the great white chief. Chikako still entertained a carnal desire to settle accounts with his immediate neighbour, the Wasanga Malamanyama. The latter, it appeared, had recovered his patrimony on the death of Msiri's nephew, Molenga, had set the king at defiance, and had even stopped several powder-caravans, under the charge of Coimbra. "Malamanyama is a very bad man," said Chikako, with a ring of righteous indignation in his voice; "his favourite occupations are murdering and stealing." However, there was another side to the story, with which I acquainted the Wanyamwesi; and, seeing that further argument might lead to yet more awkward disclosures, he signed with a shrug of philosophical resignation. Finally, Captain Stairs being ill, I made a set speech to the Msiri family on their privileges and duties, dwelling especially on the obligation to refer all disputes to the white man, and to treat their subjects with humanity. They grunted acquiescence, and withdrew; and so the settlement of the Bunkeya Valley was achieved.

During this period the fort rose slowly indeed, for many of the men were sick, and all were starving. Its shape, as designed by Captain Stairs, resembled an irregular hexagon, covering nearly an acre of ground. We first set up a double palisade of two rows of poles, fixed tightly together in the soil. The materials came mostly from Msiri's boma, and his house was also destroyed, to show all concerned that his tyranny existed no longer. (The doors, by the way, we turned to account by using them for our own huts.) Outside the fence ran a ditch four feet wide by six deep, and the excavated earth was banked against the woodwork.

The Zanzibaris hardly shone as navvies, and, the soil being heavy clay, the ditch remained unfinished by the end of the year. They were seen to better advantage in the construction of the three towers or crow's-nests, which Captain Stairs planned for the salient angles of the six-sided stronghold. These edifices comprised two storeys, and their walls consisted of wooden frameworks daubed with clay. The lower compartments, which were loopholed along two sides, formed the passages for entrance and egress, the gateways being built into their outermost fronts. The floorings of the upper chambers rested on huge forked stakes, and five uprights, one at each corner and the fifth in the centre, supported the sloping roofs. These rooms were also loopholed; and each erection would hold from eighteen to twenty men, so posted that they could fire down upon the enemy, without being themselves exposed.

So much for the defences of Fort Bunkeya; its internal arrangements were as follows. In front of the southern tower stood Captain Stairs' house, a low oblong building of timber and clay. Before the commander's dwelling we constructed, of the same materials, a large shed with two divisions: one as a store for the cloth and such European provisions as still remained, the other served for an armoury. A low paling separated this part of the fort from the remainder; and, inside the enclosure wandered our six goats, until they were converted into dead meat. In the open space beyond were placed the round tent in which *shauris* were held, the houses of the three other white men, and the flagstaff. The huts of the chiefs and men stood against the four remaining sides of the *boma*, with a narrow alley between, so that the palisade could be lined in case of attack. Each nyampara, had, of course, a cabin to himself; the rank and file were accommodated, some eight or nine together, in one of the four compartments of a hut some fifty feet long by fourteen deep. As may well be imagined, Fort Bunkeya was not built in a week, indeed the 16th of January found the men's huts still requiring a second coating of clay. However, a day or two afterwards every erection was finished; and nothing remained to be done except the demolition of the ruined native huts outside the boma, and the burning of the rubbish. The last process, by the way, nearly destroyed the whole result of our toil; as the Zanzibaris, with almost incredible carelessness, allowed some loose straw to get alight, and the flames made straight for the palisade. Fortunately an askari gave the alarm, and after a most anxious ten minutes I succeeded in stamping out the conflagration. By the end of the month Fort Bunkeya might be considered impregnable to any native enemy, even did Msiri rise from his grave, provided the soldiers would stand together. By that time, however, it had become a somewhat open question if the expedition would not be entirely wrecked by the slow but certain influences of starvation and disease.

At first the situation did not appear to be entirely desperate, though we knew, of course, from the outset that famine must be reckoned a possible eventuality. Still there were hopes that provisions would be procurable from the remoter villages which had escaped Msiri's raids, and possibly some assistance would be forthcoming from Lieutenant Legat. Accordingly the European officers of the expedition, the Marquis de Bonchamps included, sat down to their Christmas dinner in a reasonably cheerful spirit. The fare consisted of soup (Bovril), fish (tinned sardines), leg of goat, cold fowl, roast pigeon, and last, but not least, a plum-pudding, which Captain Stairs had brought all the way from the coast—"to uphold," said he, "British prestige in Katanga." He also produced a bottle of champagne; so that we had, perforce, to be jovial, though the Marquis looked terribly weak, while our host seemed possessed by a somewhat unnatural gaiety. (Robinson, by the way, remained far too ill to come out of his tent.) Still I could detect no positive sign of illness in Captain Stairs during the next few days; and he, for his part, was intent upon sending a small expedition of nine men and the small boat under my command to explore the west side of Mweru. We discussed the undertaking together for several evenings; and Stairs decided that after an investigation of the unknown shore from the point where the Luapula enters the lake, I should go to the north end and try to find Mr. Crawshay of the British Central African Administration, who, we heard, had built a station in that neighbourhood. I need hardly say that the idea of venturing into regions quite un-traversed by Europeans—for Mr. Alfred Sharpe did not go much further south than the 9th parallel—was eagerly embraced by me, but before many hours elapsed it had to be entirely abandoned. The complete circuit of Mweru still remains to be accomplished by some more fortunate traveller than myself.

On Christmas Day we became fully aware, for the first time, of the grim predicament in which the expedition was placed. Captain Stairs gave the porters a holiday, and they naturally made use of the opportunity in scouring the country far and wide for food. That night they all returned with the same story: not a mouthful to be obtained within a day's march. In the fields the natives ran away at their approach; and, on entering the villages, they discovered them absolutely destitute of provisions, and their inhabitants mere walking skeletons. Some askaris despatched to the very outskirts of the Valley came back with the same tale, though one fortunate individual secured a few handfuls of flour. Clearly the men would have to support existence upon wild vegetables until the crops ripened; and dysentery must in consequence play havoc in the ranks. As soon as their dull intelligences apprehended the full calamity, several poor wretches proceeded to desert. My boy Abdullah Mizé was among the earliest absconders, nor did Abdullah hesitate long about following his example.

Retreat, as Captain Stairs pointed out, could not be entertained for a moment, unless the expedition collapsed absolutely. We were bound by our agreement with the King of the Belgians and the Katanga Company to hold the country pending the establishment of some permanent *régime*, or the arrival of Captain Bia to our relief. For the present, then, we must endure passively, leaving the issue to Providence. Meanwhile alarms multiplied apace; since, in addition to the certainties of hostile natives and hunger, came the news that an expedition, with four white men in command, had been seen on the Luapula several weeks back. "Thomson, at last!" was the evident conclusion; and we calculated that, at the ordinary rate of progress, the explorer must have arrived within seven marches of our station. I find from my diary that the rumour reached Fort Bunkeya on the 29th of December, and the debate that night between Captain Stairs and myself was an anxious one. To him the situation presented only one solution possible: if Mr. Joseph Thomson came and tried to occupy Katanga, we must offer the most stubborn resistance in our power. True that our famished soldiery would stand a mighty poor chance against the forces of Mr. Rhodes's agent, still our engagements to King Leopold permitted no compromise of the Belgian rights as established by the conventions of 1886 and 1890. At the same time Captain Stairs thought it possible that, finding we had won the race to Msiri's capital, Mr. Thomson would quietly withdraw rather than risk international complications.

I must confess that the notion of fighting against my own fellow countrymen while receiving the pay of a foreign monarch, appeared both unnatural and repugnant. Besides, if the expedition was worsted, it could expect small mercy at the hands of Lukuku and Chikako, or, for that matter, from the Wasanga, during a retreat upon the Lualaba. Still the logic of the position comprehended no other courses except bloodshed or a tame submission; and, in any case, I had to obey the orders of my commandant. Besides, there was room for hope that we had been victimized by a false alarm; since rumour travels apace in Africa, and is singularly independent of fact. We sent for information to M. Legat upon the Lifoi, and he replied that no intelligence of the white men had reached his station. Then it occurred to us that their objective might not be Katanga at all, but the Barotse country in the British sphere. Finally, after a week's anxiety, we ascertained definitely that the caravan in our neighbourhood, was not commanded by Europeans at all, but merely by some Arabs who belonged to Kafindo's company. But before apprehensions of another Manica affair ceased to occupy our thoughts, worry and bad food had done their work with Captain Stairs, and he became dangerously ill.

On the 3rd of January, after falling in the men, and discovering that no less than a hundred and three were absent from camp in search of food, he came over and complained to me of fever. That night and the next he went through the hot and cold stages, and lost much strength in consequence. On the 5th he seemed decidedly better, his temperature being normal for the greater part of the day; and I consented to his turning out for a few hours. His constitution, however, proved unable to shake off the disease; and within a few days he developed haematuria again, becoming in consequence a mere shadow, confined absolutely to bed. Night after night I had to sit up with him, as the boys could not be depended upon to administer medicine at the proper times, or even to keep their master supplied with food. Then prolonged fainting-fits ensued, and the patient's natural restlessness aggravated his sickness. He was soon completely incapacitated from command, and I entertained the most serious doubts if he would ever reach the coast alive.

Thus, before 1892 was many days old, the whole responsibility for the expedition rested on my shoulders. Its commander was a complete invalid; the second officer, Captain Bodson, had died; the third, the Marquis de Bonchamps, was slowly recovering from a dangerous attack of fever, and quite incapable of work. Robinson, the only other European, lay at death's door from fever and starvation. The position would have tried a man in robust health and amply supplied with food; since by day the construction of the fort had to be hurried on, the sick and wounded attended, a corpse or two buried, not to mention the hundred and odd small affairs which comprise an African routine. By night the sentries had to be visited thrice, except on the rare occasions when the Marquis was well enough to take his turn; and Captain Stairs, who was terribly anxious about himself, used to summon me to his bedside at intervals of an hour or so. Yes; a strong man would have found the burden heavy enough to bear; and to one, debilitated by occasional fever and constant hunger, it proved well-nigh insupportable. How I got through the ensuing three weeks passes my powers of comprehension, and I most certainly should not care to repeat the experience. Fortunately, a naturally strong constitution and, I may fairly add, a sense of duty, carried me through.

The feelings of starvation beggar words; and almost worse than the actual pangs, was the process of forcing down the throat a diet which the stomach strongly objected to receive. It consisted of a spinach, made of leaves and grass, varied by locusts and fried white ants. The last were eaten in their winged stage, and their nastiness passes my power of description. This, with the exception of an occasional handful of flour brought by some askari from a distant village, was the only food to be had for three long weeks. It was positively painful to open one of the few remaining boxes of European provisions for the sick, who would certainly have died without their support; so strong was the temptation to appropriate the precious contents. Indeed, while feeding Captain Stairs with sardines—for he had to be nursed like a child—I was seized sometimes by an almost irresistible impulse to convey the morsel to my own mouth. Hence it can be readily imagined that my thoughts were by no means pleasant companions, and one idea, in particular, kept haunting me persistently. About seven or eight years ago an old beggar used to frequent the Strand, whom most Londoners can hardly fail to remember. He was a venerable patriarch, with a long white beard, and he never wore a hat. Well, one of his favourite devices for attracting the attention of the charitable, was that of standing outside some eating-house and gazing into the windows with anxious eyes. In my walks abroad I frequently came across the venerable mendicant thus engaged, and thinking the manoeuvre to be a trifle obvious, I never relieved his real or simulated necessities. He was avenged, however, after death, for his memory pursued me at Fort Bunkeya with a devilish malignity, and the sentence would beat a hateful tattoo upon my brain; "Why did I not give him a penny? I ought to have given him a penny."

The symptoms of African fever have frequently been set forth by travellers, and some of their accounts have been received with a certain scepticism, I remember the time when I used to doubt some of the more sensational details, particularly the illusion of duality. At Fort Bunkeya, however, the full significance of that phenomenon, as depicted by Livingstone, Cameron, and others, was very forcibly brought home to me. For days together I was attended by a second and inseparable self, who accompanied me on my rounds, used to sit opposite me when I was writing in my tent, or would pace up and down when I attempted to sleep. The irritation caused by this interloper, with his persistent efforts to take the reason prisoner, and by the resistant struggles of one's tormented intelligence, was extreme. Fortunately I had sufficient self-control to lock up my pistols, otherwise my fate might well have been that of Commander Cameron's companion, Br. Dillon, who shot himself in delirium. Also, I was able to refrain from the few remaining bottles of brandy, and from the opium with which the medicine-stores were provided. Even at the worst, one's conscience never ceased to utter the warning whisper, "Once give way, and you are lost."

Again, when free from fever, I felt oppressed by a dismal sense of loneliness and inability to exchange confidences with a living soul. As I went about the camp, I could hear Captain Stairs raving in one hut, and Robinson moaning in another; while the Marquis de Bonchamps tottered about, leaning upon his cook's arm, and utterly incapable of anything except dismal prophecies of burial far from the pleasant plains of France. The chiefs were wonderfully faithful during this time of trial, and lent me every assistance in their power. Hamadi, in particular, could be relied upon implicitly; Bedoe was slow, but sure; nor must I forget old Khamis Ngozi, though his character degenerated in a most unaccountable manner during the march to the coast. Still these men had their limitations; they would execute orders, but their advice could not be reckoned at a high value. For instance, had I attempted to consult them upon the political settlement of Katanga, the notion of imposing peace by moral suasion would have been utterly foreign to their habits of thought. Indeed Hamadi, intelligent fellow though he was, seemed perpetually at a loss to understand why we did not attack in succession Makanda Vanta, Lukuku, and Chikako, loot their villages, and appropriate their ripening harvests.

Meanwhile the men were dying at the average rate of nearly two a day. To show that this statement is no exaggeration, I will quote my case-book for a week after the famine fairly began. "Sunday, January 4, one man died from exhaustion; Monday, three men died; Tuesday, two men died; Wednesday, three men died; Thursday, two men died; Friday, two men died; Saturday, two men died." I find that during the following week eleven deaths occurred, and the same number on the third week.

In nearly every case the losses could be traced directly to want of food, through colic or inability to throw off an attack of fever. As we were now in the midst of the rainy season, when the water descended in torrents for five or six hours a day, malaria and ague naturally made their appearance. These diseases played havoc with the most enfeebled men; especially as their companions frequently left the sick to die in some out-of-the-way corner, without even troubling themselves to acquaint the "doctari" with the poor fellows' illnesses. The negligence, of course, proceeded for the most part from mere thoughtlessness; though the sentiment, "one mouth the less," undoubtedly influenced them as well.

The fact is that humanity, be it white or black, becomes mightily changed by the absence of such civilizing influences as a good dinner. While the cemetery near the camp rapidly enlarged its dimensions, I used to superintend the hasty process of placing the body in the grave, and stamping in the earth, with the utmost indifference. It became a natural part of the day's work, and there seemed nothing strange in making the report to Captain Stairs : "I have buried Suleiman-bin-Abdullah, No. 2 Company, and Juma Bakari, No. 3;" or in his answer, a matter-of-fact nod of the head. At times I used to think, "Surely this callousness cannot be natural to me; if I were in England these tragedies would not leave me completely cold." Still, all compassion seemed to have departed from my organism; all that remained was a dim consciousness of some indefinable shortcoming.

As may well be imagined, it was impossible to maintain a very rigorous discipline over a force so circumstanced. The askaris, when sent on sentry duty by night, persisted in sitting down, and, of course fell fast asleep; but Captain Stairs agreed that no severe punishment should be inflicted, as the poor devils had become terribly emaciated. Again, porters when despatched to a village some two marches off, would frequently be absent from camp for over a fortnight, and then return mere shapes of skin and bone. It was obvious, of course, that they had intended to desert, but, finding their last state in the native *tembé* worse than their first in the fort, they came back, perforce, to their duty. Sometimes they were discovered hiding in the villages by the askari who were sent to hoist the Belgian flag; thus little Abdullah Mizé was recaptured after a fortnight's absence, and promptly ran away again, as soon as occasion offered. Here again one had to accept some obvious invention about the way lost or what not; and the mildest of mild floggings was prescribed. Still these unauthorized wanderings seriously reduced the strength of the fort, which at more than one roll-call was very little over a hundred men all told. Fortunately Lukuku and Chikako did not know how we were situated.

My chief anxiety, so far as the outside world was concerned, lay in preventing the Zanzibaris from coming to blows with the natives. On the whole I succeeded beyond my expectations, though, unless rumour lied, Lukuku's men accounted for one or two of our pagazi. Makanda Vanta, on the other hand, held honourably to his engagements, and punished severely some of his subjects for raiding our young Indian corn and beans, which had been planted by the villagers before Msiri drove them forth in the previous November. (I should have mentioned, by the way, that early in January, I proceeded to lay down some two acres near the fort with wheat, lettuce, and other vegetables. The men did the hoeing, but the task of marking out the drills fell to me, since a Zanzibari cannot draw a straight line. These crops, especially the Indian corn, matured with wonderful rapidity under the tropical sun, and to them, as I shall eventually show, we owed our salvation.) The king showed an equally healthy sense of justice when one of his subjects shot a porter in the back, who had laid hands upon a basket of provisions. He handed over both the culprits, and they were sentenced to a night in the chains. Still, hungry men do not stick at trifles; and there came a time when two of our chiefs, who shall be nameless, were caught red-handed in the robbery of a native *shamba*. It was necessary to stop these excesses, so I gave them their choice of thirty-five days' confinement or a sound flogging. They looked vastly surprised, as well they might, but eventually embraced the latter alternative, and Hamadi and Bedoe laid on with a will.

Inside the camp a mutiny brewed during these arduous weeks, without coming to an actual head. The design of the malcontents was to desert in a body with their guns, and loot every village between Bunkeya and Lake Mweru, leaving the white men to shift for themselves; nor, if we offered resistance, would they have hesitated about setting the whole fort ablaze. Accordingly, a day or two before he took to his bed, Captain Stairs suddenly ordered the three companies to fall in, and deprived every man of his rifle and belt, except forty-five of the most trustworthy askaris. As porter after porter was disarmed, their mouths fell agape with absolute amazement; and so expeditiously did we act, that they had hardly grasped the situation, before the weapons were safely stacked within the store. This decisive stroke, coupled with the destruction of some forty native huts which lay outside the *boma*, which might serve therefore as nests of sedition, quelled the storm for time the being. On the 12th of January, however, Abdullah Mizé, who though an arch-absconder, was no traitor, came to me with a circumstantial account of a plot to seize the store, which he had overheard at one of the camp-fires. Who were in the business? The boy mentioned several names, and said that eight or nine askaris and some sixty pagazi had joined the conspiracy. What was their design? He heard them planning to take arms, ammunition, and cloth, and enter the service of a notorious Arab who dwelt to the south-east of Lake Mweru. Evidently the state of affairs had become very serious; and Hamadi, to whom I broached the matter, distinctly shared my opinion. We agreed to sleep outside the store by night, and arranged that some trusty chief should stand on guard by day. Accordingly for the next five nights I lay in a mackintosh at the door of the shed by the side of Hamadi. The men, finding their trick discovered gave up the idea of breaking in; and this prudent resolution received confirmation, so far as six of the ringleaders were concerned, by a most wholesome thrashing.

An occurrence next day proved that little Abdullah Mizé's disclosure was made not a moment too soon. Khamis Ngozi, his attention being on the alert, discovered the askari Ismail, two porters, and a woman, who had followed the camp from Tabora, in the act of making off with a neat little "swag". It appeared that a fortnight previously they had formed a conspiracy with Captain Stairs' boy to rob the native hut which, before his house and the shed were built, served both for the commandant's quarters and the store. The design succeeded, and the lad handed them through the window a quantity of flags, cloths, razors, scissors, and thread. So much the askari confessed; and further inquiry elicited that the woman and one of the two porters had stolen and hidden five rifles together with a hundred cartridges, procured by the same means. The rod of affliction naturally descended on the men; and the hussy was bundled out of camp, though she rejoined us, smiling, on our way to Lake Mweru. Thus, through the fidelity of the chiefs, I was able to avert an absolute outbreak, and affairs began gradually to mend.

In particular, the settlement of the country proceeded without a single hitch. When the two hundred captives, whom Msiri had condemned to death, returned to their homes, bringing with them the news of the tyrant's overthrow, the Wasanga chiefs rejoiced exceedingly. Each village began to get in its crops, and the feeling of general apprehension gradually gave place to a sense of security. For a while the famine continued to rage, but the masika rains forced on the corn and presently provisions became fairly plentiful. Accordingly, when I despatched nyamparas to the various kinglets with invitations to make acts of submission and accept the Belgian flag, they responded with alacrity. Momba and Mimba, Moensha, Molenga, and Mutwila, all hurried into the fort, accompanied by their bodyguards and wives. The usual *shauri* was held in the tent, and the ceremonial, though protracted, possessed no elaborate ritual. I would take my seat on one side, with two askaris standing on either hand; then the Sultan would be admitted together with his train. Majesty was offered a chair; his followers squatted on the ground; after which I delivered a brief discourse, setting forth the political arrangements consequent upon Msiri's death, the boundaries assigned to each chief, and the obligation to refer all tribal disputes to the white man. The reply took the form of effusive protestations of gratitude, followed by a desultory sketch of the speaker's autobiography, which it would have been a grave breach of etiquette to interrupt. The monologue having ceased from sheer physical exhaustion, the treaties would be produced, signed by the chief and myself, and witnessed by the Marquis de Bonchamps. A day or two afterwards I sent a nyampara with an escort to hoist the flag at the Wasanga's capital. In all, fifteen districts came under the settlement, and the Belgian authority was acknowledged within a radius of fifty miles from Bunkeya.

Despite their discursive tendencies, these Wasanga Sultans showed distinct intelligence, though their unwarlike dispositions must have rendered Msiri's conquests a comparatively light undertaking. Their thanks to the Stairs expedition was expressed in generous gifts of food, and in valuable information about the country. Notably, the chief Mutwila told me of a rich vein of gold to be seen close to his village, about four days' march to the south of Bunkeya. At last our hopes seemed on the point of realization, and I looked forward eagerly to the moment when Captain Stairs' recovery would permit me to visit the spot. But the fates disposed otherwise; and, after all, we returned to the coast without beholding the object of our desires.

To return to the Wasanga palavers—the *shauri* generally occupied the morning, and in the afternoon our chiefs and their wives used to give garden- parties to the visitors and their ladies, the latter generally numbering some six or seven. For hours together the camp would ring with shrill chattering and laughter; indeed, the noise rivalled that of an East End bean feast. And yet many of our poor wretches had gone without nutriment, other than grass and perhaps a handful of beans, for a week or more! Still, there they squatted in the eye of the sun, talking and gesticulating with the most unaffected gaiety. One afternoon, when Captain Stairs lay at death's door, and my own temper, I must own, was none of the sweetest, the clatter grew so unbearable that I turned the whole crew out of the fort. They took their expulsion as a matter of course, and bore me not the slightest ill-will.

Indeed, with all his faults, the Zanzibari makes a wonderfully effective pioneer to civilization in Africa. True that he has adopted the vices of the Mohammedans, with very few of the virtues proper to Islam. Thus his religion is purely imitative; and none of our chiefs even, so far as I could discover, ever said prayers, or paid a thought to the observances of Islam, beyond abstaining from food until after sunset during Ramadan. Again, the average porter is by no means nice in his person, and had the men been allowed to live according to their congenital uncleanliness, the fort would have been devastated by some epidemic in a week. Further, the Zanzibari will get drunk whenever he has a chance; his thieving propensities are a matter of common notoriety; he will desert if the slightest temptation be thrown in his way. Also he is afflicted with the negro's entire incapacity to look beyond the moment, or to carry through a protracted piece of work. In the midst of the enemy's country the porters would stare to this side and that for bananas or fruit; the askari were never on the *qui vive*. Even when the fort was being built, it was useless to tell the men, "If you do not make haste, the Wasanga will come and spear you"; was I absent for half an hour, on my reappearance every spade lay idle. Lastly, the Zanzibari invariably loses his nerve in a sudden emergency, and his instincts turn at once to flight. Yet if he will not stand by you in the hour of danger, he will aid your escape from many a grave predicament. His powers of endurance are marvellous; they defy alike hunger, cold, rain, swamps, and malaria. Nay more, when things are at their very worst, he remains the same patient and cheerful creature, accepting the situation with an easy fatalism, and entertaining no resentment towards the harshest master, provided kindliness alternate with punishment. His philosophy differs *toto coelo* from that of the ordinary European; its quiet dignity commands, nevertheless, no small amount of respect. In the end, the Briton must learn to appreciate his many merits, and to accept his shortcomings as due rather to imperfect development than to a radical wantonness of disposition.

In the second half of January the outlook brightened considerably, and I had hopes of saving the expedition. No help was forthcoming from M. Legat, who declared the waters to prevent the transport of such scanty supplies as the condition of his fort would warrant. . But the Wasanga crops had the start of ours, and as they ripened, the prospects of selling in a dear market brought many of the cultivators to Bunkeya. Also our stragglers returned, some empty-handed, but others bearing their sheaves with them. The arch-forager, Mohammed Moti, came back after a month's absence without leave; but, by way of atonement, he bore on his back a load of beans and Indian corn; and, curiously enough, the chief Suedi, who had been away for the same period, also arrived within half an hour. His contribution consisted of nine loads of *matamah* and ten fowls, for which I would have paid their weight in gold. Thus I was able to tide over the days until our Indian corn grew fairly ripe, though, had the men been left to themselves, the fields would have been laid bare before the ears formed at all. At last the heads could be cut, and then the joy of munching the roasted grain! It is quite indescribable; and, as few of my readers can have experienced prolonged hunger, I can only ask them to recall the happiest moment of their lives. From that day of blessed memory, the 24th of January, the death-rate declined until it ceased altogether; the sick-list diminished, and the men no longer tottered, but positively walked with firm footsteps.

Still the white men were ill, and two of them at death's door. Robinson, indeed, began to pick up strength, but Captain Stairs seemed quite unable to turn the corner. The haematuria continued, and pneumonia followed; while, worst signs of all, I detected tubercular symptoms, which accounted for his incapacity to shake off the fever. On the 18th he had a severe fainting-fit, and I fully expected that he would succumb about midnight, and, under the best of circumstances his rest was broken and he could take very little nourishment. In his delirium he held imaginary conversations with Mr. Joseph Thomson, and demanded his revolver, which I had fortunately secured, in order to repel that explorer. At another time he was filled with apprehensions lest the powder should catch fire, and, sending for two askaris, ordered them to shift every bag into his tent. In fact his responsibility for the expedition was never absent from his mind, and, on his better days, he listened eagerly to every detail. I noticed with admiration how, in spite of his long sickness, not a single fact had escaped his memory and how he managed to prepare for every possible contingency. The chiefs were devoted to him, and called hourly to inquire after his health. One morning he had a most affecting interview with Khamis Ngozi and five others, with whom he shook hands, and said that he felt slightly better. He told the old man how grateful he was to the nyamparas for their fidelity, and remarked that, if he died, they must regard the doctari as "Great Chief." Khamis Ngozi wept honest tears; and they all premised to stand by me, if our gravest apprehensions were realized.

Under the circumstances, I could not leave the fort, though everything stood in readiness for an expedition to the reported gold-mine near Mutwila's. Also messengers had been sent to open communications with M. Delcommune; but, after thirty-five days' absence they returned, having scoured the country to the west and south, but all in vain. Not a trace of the Belgian traveller could be discovered in any of the villages; indeed the African wastes seemed to have swallowed him up. So far as I am aware, no certain intelligence of M. Delcommune reached Brussels until, after a two years' Odyssey through Katanga and Urua, he came to the assistance of Captain Jacques on Tanganyika in July or August last. His adventures, if they are published, can hardly fail to make excellent reading; and the mere fact that he was lost to the outside world so long forms a useful illustration of the continent's vastness.

No sooner had we abandoned all hope of finding M. Delcommune, when news arrived from Captain Bia, now many weeks overdue. Indeed, I had almost ceased to think of his expedition, when, on the evening of the 29th, a messenger came into camp with a short note saying that it would reach Bunkeya next day. Accordingly, on the following morning, I started with Hamadi and some askaris to meet the caravan. After marching some ten miles, we suddenly perceived a long line of some five hundred men descending an undulation in the plain; and, as it drew nearer, a stout soldierly looking man advanced from the vanguard to meet me. This was Captain Bia, who speedily introduced me to Lieutenant Franqui, his second in command, and Doctor Amerlynck. All seemed in excellent health, and the men looked in good condition, considering how long they had been on the road. As usual, the force was composed of many nations and languages, and the Zanzibari element had by no means its usual predominance. Most of the porters came from the Lower Congo, while others had been recruited on the journey by methods closely resembling those of the old press-gang. The askari were mostly of Hausa birth, and had all the appearance of stout fighting material. Indeed, they invariably acquit themselves with credit under competent officers: for instance, those of the Royal Niger Company.

That afternoon Captain Bia occupied our old camp close to Bunkeya, and on the way I inquired the cause of his delay. It turned out that the Belgian officials on the Congo were to blame, as the caravan had been detained at Léopoldville for over two months, until the steamers arrived. Once started, the expedition encountered very few difficulties, and made several discoveries, including two large lakes as yet unnamed. The course taken was by main river to the mouth of the Sankuru, then up the stream of that tributary so far as Lusambo, whence they marched across country for seventy-two days. Captain Bia reported the road to be easy on the whole, and it would certainly appear preferable to that adopted by M. Delcommune. On the way he had two passages of arms; the first, before leaving the Sankuru, with a dependent of Tippoo Tib's, who was soon forced to cry *peccavi*. The second occurred several marches south of Lusambo, and began with a midnight attack on the camp by some sixty natives. They passed the sleeping sentries, and actually penetrated into Doctor Amerlynck's tent, when he awoke and gave the alarm. The Hausas promptly came to his rescue, and the intruders fled, bearing with them the physician's coat, which, however, they considerately dropped outside the camp. On the following day Captain Bia, by way of reprisal, burnt two villages; a proceeding, to my mind, of somewhat dubious expediency.

Chapter XIII

To Tanganyika

Captain Bia on the situation—His interview with Captain Stairs—The latter decides to return to the coast—My disappointment—Captain Bia's letter—We leave the fort—Effects of the *masika*—The death of Dick—Abdullah Mizé again—Malagarazi's truculence—Lukuku's irregulars—Illness of the white men—Disorganization of the caravan—Across the plateau—Lake Mweru—The Lualaba again—Mpweto's village—The Marquis's mishaps—More desertions—Letters from Mr. Crawshay and Herr von Siegl—Scarcity of guides—Mpweto and Kapalongo—Swamps and downs—Primitive hill-men—Wanyamwesi settlements—Through swamps to Tanganyika.

IN the afternoon Captain Bia and M. Franqui paid a visit to the fort, and seemed much pleased with the general aspect of the place. The Marquis and I entertained them at dinner to the best of our poor ability, and fortunately a present of some tinned meat from the missionaries arrived to supplement our staple fare, roast Indian corn. At the same time we beard that Messrs. Crawford and Lane had gone back to their station from M. Legat's fort, all fear of danger being completely at an end. Captain Bia naturally took deep interest in our story of the fight, the death of Captain Bodson, and the famine, none of which news had reached him on the journey. At the same time the Belgian officers seemed much surprised that we should have taken so much trouble about building the fort and settling the country. Why had we not gone south in search of gold, and left the Wasanga to stew in their juice? In fact, they seemed to think only of firing off expeditions, and the permanent administration of the district occupied a most subordinate place in their thoughts. As to the immediate future, Captain Bia evidently felt considerable perplexity; but, on hearing of the very dangerous condition of Captain Stairs' health, he decided to recommend an immediate return to the coast, and the withdrawal of the whole expedition.

With much thoughtfulness Captain Bia sent the sick man some bottles of Bordeaux and champagne, which went far to restore his strength, and for which he was extremely grateful But he could hardly sit up in bed, when Captain Bia came to discuss the pros and cons of departing or remaining. Accordingly the interview was extremely short; and, after the Belgian commandant had pointed out that the expedition had done its work and established peace in Katanga, Captain Stairs merely whispered, "Yes; you are right. I will go." Two days afterwards he expressed his reasons for acquiescence, in the following letter to Captain Bia, which I wrote at his dictation.

"Fort Bunkeya, February 3rd, 1892.

"DEAR SIR,

"I have, on deliberate consideration with my officers, decided to return to Europe with my expedition. The deposition of Msiri, the election of his successor, the restoration of tranquillity in the country, and the provisions for the future peace and happiness throughout the land, encourage me sufficiently to believe that I have done all that can be done at present, both for the Company and the country, by remaining here under the difficulties which we have encountered during the last six months.

" We arrived here, found the position a difficult one, with Msiri's word law, with famine and sickness all over the country, and we decided to act in a speedy manner, which we did, but which left us stranded from want of provisions. We remained here until your arrival, getting what best we could to eat, while planting crops which are not yet ripe. Many of our men died of hunger and sickness, and the expedition has had such a hard knock that now the only thing to be done is to march them slowly to the coast.

"Three of the white men are ill.

"Yours, etc.,

"W. G. STAIRS."

At the same time he dictated a letter to Mr. Crawford, the missionary, expressing regret for having to leave the country without seeing him again. "I am sick," he added, "Bonchamps is sick, also Robinson. Moloney is the only strong man. I have been in bed now twenty-nine days, and feel that I am not justified in remaining here any longer. Good-bye to you all, and success to your mission. Send letters rapidly to Kifuntwé's, and we will take them on."

At first, Captain Stairs wished me to remain at Fort Bunkeya, with a small detachment, while Captain Bia explored the surrounding country. I felt, however, that it was my duty to accompany the safari, at least into British territory, where Captain Stairs could be placed in a competent doctor's hands; and the Belgian officers entirely shared my opinion. Indeed, he was far too ill to travel alone, while Robinson would have to be carried every yard of the distance, and M. de Bonchamps could barely walk five miles a day. Accordingly, it was decided that I must accompany the return march, though my own desires emphatically leant to my chief's original proposal. Indeed, I felt bitterly mortified that, having toiled night and day, without any one in whom to confide my troubles, at building the fort, sowing the crops, and settling the country, the Belgians should step in and annex the results of my labours. An easy task lay before them; as the Indian corn was ripening rapidly, the valley had become absolutely peaceful, and the mines could be explored at leisure. More over, Bunkeya had become very dear to me after so much suffering and anxiety; it was almost a second home. I had to turn my back upon the familiar boma, and escort an expedition of three sick men, and porters still enfeebled by fevers and starvation, through swamps and rivers to Lake Mweru. The bolus stuck in my throat; but, under the circumstances, my lot, as medical officer, evidently lay with my invalided leader. How far Captain Bia was well-advised in recommending an immediate retreat, was by no means clear to my mind. I could not help thinking that the journey might well have been postponed for a few months, until the waters had subsided, and, with them, had disappeared the deadly morning mists. However, Captain Stairs had decided otherwise, and the die was cast. Nothing remained but to obtain from Captain Bia some acknowledgment for my conduct of affairs since the illness of our first and second in command.

Accordingly, I wrote a letter, setting forth the story of Fort Bunkeya and its attendant episodes. Captain Bia sent me the following reply, dated the 4th of February:—

"SIR,

"I have just received your letter, dated from Fort Bunkeya, in which you ask for my personal opinion on the works you have carried out. I have learnt, with pleasure, that during the long illness of your commander, Captain Stairs, and the constant fevers of the Marquis de Bonchamps, you have occupied your time, not only with the construction of the fort, which, indeed, is most admirably planned, but also with political affairs. I am glad to bear witness to your exertions.

"You are compelled to leave Bunkeya, both in obedience to your commander's orders, and in accordance with the dictates of your duty, and of the affection, which you bear towards him. You can leave Bunkeya with the feeling that you have never swerved from your task. For my own part, I can but congratulate you upon the results achieved."

That afternoon I dined with the Belgian officers, and partook of the first meat that had passed my lips since Christmas Day, the missionaries' present excepted. The verb "to eat" assumed, thenceforth, an entirely new significance in my vocabulary.

The work of getting ready for the start taxed my best energies, but, on the 4th, at 8.30 a.m., the procession wound out of Bunkeya. The caravan had been reduced from some three hundred and sixty to two hundred, during that terrible month of January, of whom seventy-three had been laid to rest in the cemetery, and the remainder were still wandering in the wilderness. Accordingly, the adjustment of the loads was no easy matter; and we had to leave behind a considerable quantity of ammunition, together with the smaller steel boat, for which Lieutenant Franqui, who took over the fort in the name of Captain Bia, gave me a receipt. After a cordial farewell from that pleasant young Belgian officer, I hurried after the caravan. It was soon caught up, as the porters, being still very weak, could make neither fast nor long marches. Besides, the Marquis de Bonchamps, after a plucky attempt to keep on his legs, had to take to a hammock, and thereby took six strong men away from the loads. So we crawled across the plain of Bunkeya, and made for Malagarazi's village.

It soon became evident that the return from Katanga would be a more difficult undertaking than the journey thither. At first we flattered ourselves that the *masika* had finally passed away, but two or three downfalls of torrential rain soon undeceived us on that account. And already the wet season had entirely altered the face of the country, so that even bold landmarks could be recognized with difficulty. Thus flats formerly bare were covered with grass knee-high, and what was before a pleasant plain had now become a pestiferous swamp. Even under favourable circumstances, progress was naturally slow; and there were days during which the men bad to wade continuously through water, which the long reeds kept icy cold, while the burning sun beat down on their beads. As may be well imagined, the sick-list rose with a bound, and we had to leave several porters behind in the villages, who were too debilitated to travel. Indeed, one or two deaths actually occurred, notably that of poor Dick, a pagazi, who was a general favourite. He had served in the Emin Relief Expedition, and had gained great esteem with us as a hard-working and well-conducted young fellow. Unfortunately, he had by no means shaken off the effects of short commons; and one day, as we were marching through an endless swamp, he was overcome by an irresistible desire to rest. Accordingly, he stole aside into the bamboos until the rear-guard had passed, intending to follow at his leisure. However, the cold caught him and he died. Dick's absence went undiscovered until we reached camp, when a party was sent back to bring him in. They found the body peacefully reposing on a small hillock, with the load at its feet. And there, far from his native Mombasa, the faithful porter was left to rot unburied.

By way of compensation for these outward losses we picked up several deserters, who, having fared indifferently at the hands of the natives, gladly rejoined the expedition, with the usual assortment of plausible excuses. Among them was Abdullah Mizé; who, however, attempted no evasions, but calmly informed me that he re-entered my service not from good-will, but simple necessity. Malagarazi's people, it appeared, had beaten and starved him, so that he might just as well have remained at Bunkeya; which story he related with a frank unconcern that went far to disarm my wrath. For several weeks after his reinstatement, Abdullah Mizé conducted himself with unwonted steadiness and propriety. Then the young savage's love of liberty waxed uncontrollable, and he deserted again—this time never to return. What region of the vast continent now holds that bold, if unscrupulous, spirit I know not; and neither Abdullah nor little Mizé Pharo could refrain from the dubious joys of desertion during the hard times which followed. In truth Zanzibari boys are born adventurers, and both kindness and severity fail to curtail their innate love of wandering.

Already we experienced the very different reception awaiting a weak caravan in retreat, and that accorded to the same force in full career of success. Whereas the *ruga-ruga* had prudently left us alone when we passed through the same country three months previously they now dogged the caravan in the most pertinacious fashion, and showed every disposition to spear straggling porters for the sake of their loads. These men owed allegiance to the old scoundrel Lukuku, who evidently wished to pay off old scores by harassing our departure. Moreover Malagarazi, near whose village we encamped for three days to rest the expedition, was far more untractable than on the occasion of our first encounter. He flatly refused to let our men cross to his larger village, which was built on an island, saying that we should starve before his people sold us food. This churlish non-intercourse the chief emphasized by removing the canoes which served to convey passengers across the ferry. As he was plainly acting in conjunction with Lukuku, and the pair evidently meditated mischief I retorted that if Malagarazi displayed hostile intentions the white men would burn the village about his ears. Where- upon he relented, and not only gave our men free passage, but sent a reluctant present of flour and a small kid. We parted, therefore, on fairly amicable terms, but Lukuku's irregulars still hung in our rear, and three of them cut off a pagazi, who was in charge of Captain Stairs' goat, and compelled him by threats to surrender the beast. A nyampara and two askaris were sent back to Malagazari's, whither the robbers had taken refuge; and he, after some demur, delivered them over, though one made his escape. I held a court-martial on the two captives—Captain Stairs being too ill to be worried with the affair—and our chiefs to a man were of opinion that they must die, otherwise the *ruga-ruga* would pursue the expedition for weeks together. Accordingly Hamadi and I took Lukuku's men outside the camp, and shot them there. That night hardly an eye was closed, as we fully expected to be attacked by the Wasanga in overwhelming masses. However, the severe example had taught them discretion, and from that day forward the ruga-ruga troubled us no more. The execution of the prisoners savoured, no doubt, of brutality; but I am convinced that, had they been pardoned, the *safari* would never have reached Lake Mweru, still less Zanzibar.

So we proceeded on our melancholy pilgrimage, the only cheerful circumstance being the health of Captain Stairs, which lowly but perceptibly acquired tone. But the Marquis de Bonchamps had a bad relapse, and on the 14th I was attacked by haematuric fever. For the best part of a week I thought each night would be my last, though the mornings brought a certain amount of relief. However, I may fairly say that I stuck to the rear-guard until absolute weakness forced me to take to a litter. The incidents of that terrible time present them- selves in a strange medley of hallucination and reality, to which a remarkably incoherent diary affords very little elucidation. I remember sitting, with aching head, back, and legs, on the bank of the Lufira, and attempting to direct the fitting together of the *Blue Nose* by Hamadi and four askaris. Next day the crossing seemed as if it would never end, as, in addition to the safari, we transported some forty natives, who were travelling with us for protection. As the white men's supervision no longer kept the caravan in order, discipline became sensibly relaxed. Thefts from the loads were numerous, and old Khamis Ngozi, who had evidently wearied of the whole affair, was caught red-handed with a quantity of stolen cloth. Moreover a suspiciously abundant quantity of food appeared every night in camp; and there can be little doubt, I fear, that the porters, with the connivance of the chiefs, must have looted the neighbouring villages. Captain Stairs had certainly given the strictest orders to the contrary; but as he, the Marquis, and myself all lay supine, such commands soon became a dead letter. Still consolation was derived from the circumstance that our heroes began to put on flesh apace, and, owing to the strength supplied by corn and beaus, made long and rapid marches.

Proceeding along our former road, we reached Kifuntwé's on the 19th, and so past Maroa's to Kifambula's, outside whose village we encamped on the 5th of March. Day after day we tramped through grass some seven feet high, or foundered through swamps; night after night the rain descended, and frequently delayed the start until close upon noon. With temperatures at 102° or even higher, none of the white men could boast the best of tempers; but somehow we managed to suit one another's humours, though the Zanzibaris hardly conduced to serenity by letting fall the hammocks some ten times a day. The passage of the Luvule, however, was effected without difficulty by bridge and ford, Captain Stairs being so much stronger that he was able to sit in a chair and superintend the operation. Then we crossed the plain of Chewella again, but found it changed from a meadow covered with winding streams to a swamp waist-deep in water. On the 9th we encamped near the village of our acquaintance Uturutu, whose hospitality was grossly abused by two of our soldiers. They had been gone forward on the previous day, without permission and, proceeded to demand a present of eggs and fowls on the plea that the great chief was very ill. It is hardly necessary to say that the gift disappeared down their own gullets, and Captain Stairs only discovered the imposition from an accidental remark of the Arab's. After some difficulty the culprits were discovered, and a salutary punishment inflicted. Soon afterwards we crossed the Luvule for the last time, and struck across the high plateau overlooking the north-west corner of Lake Mweru. This country is covered for the most part with scanty forest, and stands some five thousand feet above the sea-level. It appeared sparsely populated and the inhabitants looked upon all strangers as probable enemies, so that guides were with difficulty obtained. We understood this timidity on reaching a village called Parasonga. It had been raided and burnt by a Swahili scoundrel, Simba by name, who returned to his headquarters, about an eight hours' march away, with slaves galore. A miserable remnant, after wandering disconsolate through the woods, had come creeping back to its ruined homestead by twos and threes. We left them placidly resigned to their losses, and even preparing to rebuild.

  The caravan came along the level in gallant style, and on the 15th we sighted Lake Mweru. Though the maps exaggerate its size considerably; this is a fine sheet of water, and must measure quite twenty miles across, from the point at which we struck the rim. Both sides were surrounded by steep bluffs some two hundred feet above the level, and our guide must needs take us down a nearly perpendicular descent to a small fishing village on the shore. We arrived, after many stumbles and collisions, only to discover that we ought to have kept along the brow and encamped at a large village owned by Chipula, Mpweto's brother. Next day we had to ascend again after an hour's wallowing in a swamp; accordingly the comments on that guide hardly assumed the form of benedictions. Still the journey across the highland had done us all much benefit; Captain Stairs could actually stand on his feet, Robinson was recovering, and I was able to resume command of the rearguard, which had latterly been left to its own devices. We marched therefore along the crest of the cliff in excellent spirits, and reached a deserted village on the south bank of the Lualaba, just where the river issues from the lake. It runs, from that point due west for about two hundred yards, then takes a sharp curve to the south-west, and must effect further bends before reaching Ngwena's, where its current flows due north. The *Blue Nose* was soon put together, the natives readily supplied canoes, and as the porters had at last begun to fall into their places, the Lualaba was re-crossed on the 18th without a single hitch.

A six-mile march brought us to a *shamba* outside Mpweto's village, where the expedition was destined to halt until the 23rd. The reason for this stay was that Captain Stairs wished to confer with Mr. Crawshay of the Central African Administration as to the line of demarcation between British and Belgian territory and our speediest route to the coast; and with the Arab Kapalongo, who was constantly harrying Mpweto and enslaving his people. Our old friend received us with the utmost cordiality; but his medicine-man surveyed Captain Stairs with looks of ineffable scorn, and absolutely declined a renewal of the acquaintance, to our intense amusement. The village was well situated, and must have contained some eight hundred inhabitants. In fact, there was a time when Mpweto exercised a very considerable sway, but latterly his power has been circumscribed by the Arabs, and he has bent to avoid breaking. His people looked well-nourished, but their food supply was sadly limited. They had plenty of sweet potatoes and *matamah*, but no fish or fowls, and very little honey. Hence, while the Zanzibaris waxed fat, the convalescent white men pined for a change of diet.

It was terribly dull work waiting for Mr. Crawshay, as, besides a little fishing, the neighbourhood offered few attractions by way of sport, and the rain descended pitilessly. One morning the Marquis set out to survey the north end of Mweru; but his guides led him astray, and he returned after a day's wandering in the wilderness, without having seen the water at all. Soon after his reappearance, M de Bonchamps was evicted from his tent by a column of white ants. As he lay on his bed, he perceived the enemy advancing, and attempted to divert the invasion by dumping a box in its way. Instantly the insects spread all over the place, got under his clothes, and bit him so severely that he had, perforce, to shift his quarters for the night. We lit fires all round the tent, and in the morning the plague was stayed.

The men evidently felt the tedium, as they were longing to return to Zanzibar; and Khamis Ngozi completed the catalogue of his iniquities by deserting. He had been on the black list for repeated thefts, so that we were not altogether sorry when he repaired to Ngwena's with the idea of making his way home through Karema and Tabora. Abdullah Mizé promptly followed his example, though I had fed and clothed him since his reappearance, as a mere skeleton, at Malagarazi's. It was not until many weeks afterwards that a possible clue was forthcoming to this apparently ungrateful conduct. The boy was alleged to be—not freed as I had imagined—but the slave of a peculiarly harsh master at Zanzibar to whom he feared to return. Somehow the story lacked plausibility; still, Abdullah Mizé had behaved so faithfully at Fort Bunkeya, that I should be sorry to think him a simple malingerer.

Late on the evening of the 22nd, a messenger arrived with a long letter from Mr. Crawshay. He had been shooting in the *pori*, and thus our askari failed to discover his whereabouts; and now arrears of business, together with famine and mutiny at his station, prevented an expedition to Mpweto's. However, he sent Captain Stairs a full account of Mr. H. H. Johnston's exploits against the Arab chiefs, Kasembé and Makanjira, at the south end of Lake Nyasa, together with a description of the reverse in which poor Captain Maguire was killed. He added that Mr. Johnston was now at the lower part of the lake with all his steamers, and that the war might be considered at an end. This news hardly pleased Captain Stairs; as we might find ourselves completely at a loss for convoy, and the hostilities might have prevented the annual sowing, so that we should advance into a hungry country swarming with angry Arabs. Accordingly we might be compelled, after all, to return to the coast by Karema, Tabora, and Ugogo, which journey of over eight hundred miles would mean marching until December at least. But next day Mr. Crawshay forwarded our mails, including letters from home, some English newspapers, nearly a year old, but none the less precious, and—what was of more immediate import—a communication from Herr von Siegl. That undaunted soldier held out little hope of a safe return through Tabora. He made light, as usual, of his own position, but said that the tribes between his head-quarters and Bagamoyo were again on the war-path. The Wagogo had cut a caravan to pieces, and the Wahéhé had massacred a German expedition commanded by Lieutenant Zelewski near Mpwapwa.

Accordingly, nothing remained, but to take the chances and pursue our original route, via Tanganyika, the Stevenson road, and Nyasa. At the outset we had great difficulty in obtaining guides, as the natives did not care to go far from their villages, lest they should be killed while returning. Again, we had some difficulty in making them understand our intentions; and, owing to the number of Europeans in the land, the customary formula, "Take me to the white man," availed not at all. At one time Captain Stairs thought of steering by compass across country, and risking *pori* and mountains. However, guides were forthcoming at last; and, without waiting for Kapalongo, we set out on the 24th through swamps to the river Lukinda.

Arrived at the Lukinda, we discovered it to be a deep muddy stream about thirty yards wide and swarming with crocodiles. As the current ran like a mill-race, the askaris had considerable difficulty in getting the rope across, but after some duckings the feat was accomplished, and the safari passed over. Captain Stairs crossed in the *Blue Nose*, which I had put together on the previous evening; and then I had to return for Kapalongo, who came with Mpweto to keep his appointment thus tardily. The pair arrived with some forty followers apiece, and Kapalongo proved to be a thickset Swahili nigger, calling himself Arab, but with little or no Semitic blood in his veins. However, he brought a present of fowls and eggs to supplement a somewhat hazy expiation of his delays, and answer the questions put to him by Captain Stairs with shrewdness and pertinence. Indeed in the *shauri* Mpweto was reduced to a wholly secondary part, and contented himself by endorsing his more fluent companion's remarks by grunts indicative of intense admiration. In fact, the complete ascendancy obtained over the common black, by anything calling itself Arab, could not have been more strikingly displayed; more especially when one remembered that the two had been at variance for many years and that the immigrant had actually annexed several of Mpweto's villages. To ourselves Kapalongo displayed a mouth grinning with amiability, and readily gave Captain Stairs letters of introduction to his various friends along the road. The *shauri* over, Mpweto and his braves were ferried across the

Lukinda, and went home after a most ceremonious farewell. Kapalongo's band went ahead to his village, outside which he stood next morning to receive us as we marched past. The man's character may have been indifferent, indeed hideous stories were in vogue as to his methods of warfare; but we felt at liberty to credit him with the outside attributes of a gentleman.

The first of Kapalongo's friends, another Swahili, was away on business, which occupation, we heard comprised the conveyance of a caravan of slaves to Tabora, in the heart of German territory. Comment is superfluous; but, the affair being none of ours, we proceeded along a road which on the high-ground made good walking—except for tall grass, which cut the face, now and again, like whip-cord, and even threatened the eyes—but which in the plains led us through swamps thigh-deep, with for variety, a hole up to your necks. The Lukinda kept reappearing with the persistence of a reputable relation, and had to be crossed now by ford and again by boat. Moreover, the *masika* rains still fell, though by rights they should have ceased long before we reached Mpweto's. In summer-time these valleys are doubtless smiling meadow-land; in March they reeked of miasma and decay; while villages being entirely absent, despite signs of former occupation, our men had to put up with half rations and afterwards with none. On the last day of the month we got into mountain country, traversed by little torrents; and then we crossed stretches very like our own South Downs. In fact, could the nigger element have been eliminated from the scene, you might have imagine yourself walking from Brighton to the Dyke. The first part of this stage, with its rapid gradients, tried the pagazi very much, more especially as they were faint from want of food. Some crept into the grass and had to be routed out; others threw down their loads, and declined to proceed. Also a deadlock occurred at each stream; and as we crossed some fifteen a day, the rear-guard altogether was anything but a sinecure. Thefts from the bales, too, continued rife; until Captain Stairs ordered the whole caravan to fall in, and delivered a severe lecture upon picking and stealing, which, combined with a little corporal punishments bore salutary fruit.

On the 2nd of April, matters improved, as we reached a *shamba* where the natives had some goats, sweet potatoes and a little Indian corn for sale. The fare hardly meant luxury, but to men who had been for two days without provender it was an absolute godsend.

These savages seemed a most curious set of very primitive hillmen. Their ignorance of the outside world was complete, and none appeared aware that a vast sheet of water, called Tanganyika, lay but a few miles away. Our arrival caused at first a general stampede to the rocks, from which vantage-ground they peered with alarmed curiosity; but eventually the desire for barter prevailed, and the bolder spirits descended. Within their little territory they led a semi-nomadic existence, due to intertribal wars. Their corn was grown upon the mountainside, and close to the rude field stood a group of flimsy stick-huts, which a puff of wind might well have blown away. These *kibandas* were few in number, some five or six at most; no villages nor permanent buildings of any kind could be seen. Accordingly, on the approach of more powerful enemy, the small community has but to retreat through the bush, build fresh shanties, hoe a new patch of land and start life afresh. A provisional kind of existence truly; but one nevertheless with which its devotees appeared thoroughly contented.

Next our road led through mountains covered with trees, until, on the 8th, we came to some Wanyamwesi settlements. The Arabs, we heard, had driven these emigrants so far to the south of their native land; but they retained in exile all their old customs, and dwelt in large villages constructed on the Unyanyembe pattern, with large circular boma. In the capital, so to speak, there ruled a boy-chief, Laméwa by name, whom we found to be a nephew of our old friend Seke. We also learnt that there had been a famine in the land, Laméwa's *tembé* having lost a hundred persons from hunger. However, the tribes to the north suffered far more, and already Wanyamwesi industry had gone far to repair the mischief. Food abounded, and was sold at reasonable prices. Indeed, during the next few days we passed through a succession of large shambas, which came to an end with the limit of the colony. Everywhere these intelligent husbandmen gave us the greatest assistance; particularly during the passage of the river Choma, whose strong stream so alarmed our headman, Bedoe, that he declined to take the rope across. Two Wanyamwesi, whose curiosity led them to the spot, promptly put the Zanzibari to shame, and thus the passage of the turbulent stream was effected. If the civilization of East Africa ever gets translated into fact, the Wanyamwesi will doubtless come to be reckoned among the most progressive elements in the new society.

Emerging from New Unyanyembe on the 12th, we entered an appalling series of swamps, with the sun beating like a steam-hammer on our heads, and the mosquitoes biting with fiendish pertinacity. In one place I remember the water covered the taller men to their shoulders, and the shorter to their mouths; indeed, my cook, who was exceptionably little of stature, at times disappeared altogether. However, they floundered through somehow, and, by an inexplicable process, managed to keep the loads on their heads. One or two causalities indeed occurred; thus a poor pagazi, who was rather out of sorts, suddenly went under with his bale atop, and, but for prompt assistance, would most certainly have been drowned. By way of variety, we experienced a sharp earthquake, after pitching camp that night (the 14th). The motion was from north to south, and for twenty seconds the tents rocked as though in a fresh gale.

Chapter XIV

To the Coast

Muini Mtelika's—Captain Stairs starts in the *Blue Nose*—Kabunda's—Kinyamkola—-News of Captain Jacques—Crossing the Saisi—The French mission at Mambwé—Fife—Captain Stairs' instructions—My forced march to Karonga's—Through swamp and over mountain—Yarafua Brahim's letter—My black companions—Karonga's—The Wangoni and Wa-Nkonde— Arrival of the expedition—On board the *Domira*—Mandara's mishap—Mr. and Mrs. McCalmont—Jumbi and his wives— Mponda's—The Sarifi business—Within the malaria belt— Vicenti—The men get drunk—Captain Stairs' illness and death—His burial—Conclusion.

NEXT day our troubles ceased, as some dry down-country intervened between the hills overlooking Tanganyika. After a three hours' march, we climbed the heights, and beheld once more the lake two thousand feet below; though, somehow, the enthusiasm displayed on the former occasion hardly prevailed among the wayworn company. Possibly the comparative tameness of the scene, as compared with Mount Mrumbi, was to blame; at any rate, when we encamped that night, the Zanzibaris testified to their general content by a prodigious beating of drums, which continued for the space of three hours. Indeed, the spot was calculated to evoke feelings of satisfaction from organisms even less buoyant. We rested outside a large village owned by Muini Mtelika, a Swahili Sultan and slave-dealer, who owns allegiance to the great Tippoo Tib. There is little to be said about his appearance, which was that of a fat coast-nigger; and his immediate retainers also claimed Swahili origin, though their numerous slaves were recruited from the neighbourhood, the countries, namely, of Itawa and Urungu. The Sultan has amassed considerable wealth by trading in slaves with Ujiji; and his settlement, variously called Sumbo and Msika, showed ever y evidence of prosperity. The whole surface of the narrow valley was laid out in groves of bananas and fields of rice, *matamah*, and

Indian corn, wherewith our porters gorged themselves to their hearts' content. That evening the whole population hearing that there was a "doctari" in camp, appeared for treatment, headed by Muini Mtelika, who complained of rheumatism. I treated over a hundred for divers sicknesses, some real but many imaginary, till the medicine-stock threatening emptiness, the remainder were sent unphysicked away.

That evening Captain Stairs—who, though able to walk, was still far from well—decided to embark in the *Blue Nose* and coast round the southern shore to Abercorn, leaving the Marquis de Bonchamps in command of the caravan. He started on the 17th, and next day M. de Bonchamps led the way through some terribly stiff bush, in which loads were capsized by overhanging branches, and five perverse goats caused endless trouble. Avoiding the more prominent headlands, we kept, otherwise, close to the lake, and the 20th found us at Kabunda's, in the valley of the Lofu. To that river we descended a steep bad road; and there met Captain Stairs, who had ascended from its mouth in the *Blue Nose* and, with his accustomed energy, had already passed the rope across. Kabunda was away, according to the official explanation, on a family visit to Ujiji; but unauthorized rumour stated him to be on a slave-dealing journey. However, he bears a very fair reputation; and the valley of the Lofu, with its numerous villages and well-cultivated enclosures, testified to a certain genius for administration. From his factotum, a gaunt Swahili, we received every attention; and a native sub-chief appeared with a most generous present of provisions, for which we were most thankful, with three days' *pori* before us. His subjects were by no means given to equal hospitality; on the contrary, some of them robbed our pagazi, and a mighty to-do broke out in the small hours, which necessitated an armed intervention. In fact, these people at the south end of Tanganyika seemed inordinately prone to pilfering and scarce a village did we pass through but quarrel ensued owing to the theft of a gun or some cloth. Thus the start from Muini Mtelika's was delayed by the discovery that a rifle had been stolen from one of the askari. The Sultan, however, after some demur, had the gates shut and the place searched, with the result that the secreted weapon was discovered and the culprit punished.

For two days we traversed a high plateau some two thousand three hundred feet above the lake's level, and quite five thousand above the sea. On the 24th, however, we descended again to the shore, which we hit at Pambete Bay. Next a most romantic march at sunrise took the caravan to the English mission station at Kinyamkola There we again found Captain Stairs waiting for us, together with Dr. and Mrs. Mathers, and Mrs. Swann of the London Missionary Society. Mr. Swann, much to our regret, was away at Ujiji, where Rumiliza, with that generous chivalry which characterises the Arab, bad given permission for a consignment of stores to pass through. From his wife, however, and from Dr. and Mrs. Mathers as well, we received kindness which I, for one, shall never forget; and great was the pleasure of sitting in an European house for the first time since our departure from Bagamoyo. In other respects our stay at that thriving settlement was hardly enjoyable, as the heat by day rendered the slightest exertion almost unendurable, and by night great storms arose which threatened to uproot the tent-pegs.

Since we had entered British territory, everything seemed to prosper with the expedition. On the 27th Captain Stairs rejoined us, a few hours before we arrived at the African Lakes Company's station at Kituta or Abercorn, looking none the worse for his grilling in the *Blue Nose*, during which he had amused himself and caught many fish by "railing" with a boathook. Our reception by the company's representatives, Messrs. Andrew Law and Yule, was hospitality itself; and we could not but admire the immense progress achieved since the fort was established by Mr. H. H. Johnston in 1889. Abercorn, however, has been described by so many pens, that I need not dilate upon its thriving trade with various parts of Tanganyika, Itawa, and Urungu, nor on its importance from the strategic point of view. We were sorely loth to quit so pleasant a spot; but Captain Stairs, now that he had become convalescent, was for pushing forward with all possible speed. I think that the news which had come down the lake may have increased his anxiety to reach the coast, for it was of the most dismal kind. Captain Jacques, it seemed, had suffered a reverse at the hands of the Manyuema, in which his third in command, the unfortunate M. Vrithoff, had been captured, and afterwards eaten by those bloody-minded cannibals, his scalp and a few fingers excepted. Also we heard that Rumaliza, though he had condescended to accept the appointment of Governor of Ujiji from the Germans, had sworn to exterminate the white men, and would probably begin by settling accounts with Captain Jacques and M. Joubert. At the same time the fiery Arab sent a leopard cub as a present to Her Majesty Queen

Victoria, which Captain Stairs brought with him when he joined the *safari* two days from Abercorn, where he had been detained by business. It was an exceptionally fine specimen, but it died, unfortunately, during the voyage home.

I need not dwell at length on the journey between Tanganyika and Nyasa, as the famous Stevenson road, along which we travelled, has been described by numerous pilgrims, official and private. We were soon three thousand feet above the former lake again, and tramping through a cold atmosphere which acted on the nerves like wine. On the 29th we encamped at the village of Fwambo, about three miles from the English mission station, having previously passed the French mission at Zombé, which, however, lay too far off the path for a visit. On the 1st of May we arrived at the Saisi, a river with a big swamp or ooze on either side. Here considerable delay occurred, as, on attempting to cross by the frail bridge, the men carrying Captain Stairs and Robinson let them both into the water, so that they were wet through. Fortunately, neither suffered any damage beyond a ducking, and, the invaluable *Blue Nose* being put together, they eventually got over without further accident. Still, the passage of so much water cut nearly the whole day to waste; and one unlucky porter foundered with his load, containing Robinson's bed and some English flour, which were completely spoilt. Also the mosquitoes tormented the men during the two hours' halt in a manner well-nigh incredible. As for the Europeans, they had to keep attendants by them waving branches to and fro, otherwise the would have been no staying in the place. Next day we crossed a much smaller river without the slightest mishap, and on the 3rd reached the French mission station of Mambwé. The Fathers had only occupied the post five months; but already they had erected the buildings, grown and reaped a crop of wheat, and planted a large garden with vegetables. After excellent progress for two days through *pori*, we attained on the 6th the African Lakes Company's station of Mwenzo or Fife. Mr. McCullough, who was in charge, received us most kindly, and Captain Stairs was much impressed by the strength of the fort, which had been built some two years previously. It stood square, with a stiff palisade surrounded by a very deep ditch, and seemed quite impregnable to native attack.

From Fife Captain Stairs ordered me to proceed by forced marches to Karonga's, on Nyasa, and to arrange for the expedition's shipment down the lake. I give his instructions, as drawn up on the previous day, since they exemplify, better than any language of mine, his capacity for organization and aptitude for command.

"Camp, Myranmanga River, May 5th, 1892.

"DEAR SIR,

"Tomorrow (6th) the expedition should arrive at Mwenzo. I wish you on the following day to start from that place with ten men and march as quickly as possible to the African Lake Company's station at Karonga's. Take with you only such light articles as are absolutely necessary, and no load should be over thirty pounds in weight, except the small tent (Robinson's) which you will take.

"On arrival at Karonga's, make such arrangements as are necessary for the transport of four Europeans and one hundred and seventy-five blacks down Lake Nyasa in the S.S. *Domira*. These arrangements are simple. But I wish to know from you on arrival—

"1. The cost per head of Europeans on the steamer.
"2. The cost per head for blacks when the African Lakes Company feeds them on board the steamer.
"3. The cost per head for blacks should they be fed by the expedition.
"4. The price per ton to south end of lake for freight.
"5. Whether it is possible, in the event of the men being paid as in 3, that the steamer should stop somewhere for sufficient time to allow the men to get food. I need not say that 3 would be the best and cheapest for us.

"Also inquire if the Karonga agent would be willing to buy the steel boat *Blue Nose* at £75.

"I trust that the expedition will arrive at Karonga's on the 14th instant, and it would be ready to embark the same evening should such be necessary.

"As you are going light, I expect you to average twenty English miles per day. A guide will be given you, but the following camps are given for your information.

"Mwenzo to Kapakolo (1).
"Kapakolo to Nyumbo (2).
"Nyuinbo to Miniwanda's (3).
"Miniwanda's to Lufira (4).
"Lufira to Karonga's (5).

"Should you meet with our couriers on their way back from Karonga's, please hurry them on so that I may get from them any information they possess.

"I have asked that the steamer be delayed for us till the 15th instant. Should she have sailed, please remain at Karonga's till our arrival.

"Faithfully yours,
"W. G. STAIRS."

"P.S.—You should take a piece of cloth with you in case of need for food for yourself and men."

Reinforced by an excellent breakfast at Mr. McCullough's, I started at 5.50 a.m., and, pushing on through Kapakolo, which we passed at 11 a.m., halted for a rest at 12.15. When the tyranny of the midday sun had ceased, we set out again at 4 p.m. and plodded along until 7.30, when we halted for the night at the village of Panzia. In this first stage we covered over thirty-three miles; no such bad performance, considering we had some swamps to wade which were waist-deep. Next day we still kept to the plains until late in the afternoon—the guide having selected a shorter route than the Stevenson—when we began to ascend a mountain and crossed a rocky and difficult pass at 7 p.m. As the moon shone brightly, I determined to proceed; though the Zanzibaris were sorely afraid of travelling at night, as they imagined each bush to hold an enemy. However, none appeared; indeed, on reaching the village of Chitipa at nine o'clock, the chief gave us a most welcome present of flour and beans. We were off again on the third day with the dawn, and hit the Stevenson road at 9.30 near Miniwanda's, continuing, with the usual midday rest, until 7.30. As we passed the village, men and women could be seen running about, beating their breasts, and behaving as though distraught; the chief, we heard, had died that day. Further on the way I met a native with a letter for Captain Stairs, in which I enclosed a short note describing my progress, and presently encountered one of our askaris, who was returning from Karonga's. I was anxious to reach the Lufira that night, whereby a day would have been gained from the five arranged. But about five miles south of the Chamba the men showed such evident signs of exhaustion, that I was forced to call a halt, and we encamped in the *pori*.

The Lufira was crossed after an hour and a half's march on the 10th, and we began to ascend again. The top of the pass we achieved at 8.30, and there lay Nyasa at our feet, looking curiously minute amidst its tumbled surroundings, notably the mighty Livingstonian range on the eastern side. The men shouted for joy, and we hurried forward, hoping to reach Karonga's that night. But a rain-storm spoilt our calculations, added to which the road was blocked by landslips. Hence we had to clamber along the mountain side for ten yards at a time, with mighty little foothold, and a fall of some three hundred feet below. This last experience knocked all the spirit out of the porters, gallantly though they had stuck to their work; and I was forced to encamp in a *shamba* some three hours off Karonga's.

The last stage proved easy enough, as we speedily emerged from the hills and crossed the smiling plain that fringes Lake Nyasa. Our path ran through large fields of *matamah*, and across clearings upon which pastured large herds of cattle tended by Wa-Nkonde boys. Across the Lukulu, a river about one hundred feet wide, I held a hasty shauri with some Swahilis, one of whom pretended a distressing cough rather than go undoctored. At the same time the head of the settlement, one Yarafua Brahim, bribed one of the porters to convey a letter to the great chief Jumbi, whose acquaintance we were to make on the lake, announcing that a consignment of slaves was about to travel overland to the latter's village. Fortunately the pagazi, elated by so important a mission, could not hold his tongue for many days. Captain Stairs compelled him to surrender the missive, and as we possessed a Swahili scholar among the men, the neighbourly arrangement received a decisive check. However, Yarafua Brahim's negotiation passed unnoticed for the time being; and, without further adventure, we attained Karonga's about midday, where I was met by Mr. Taylor and Mr. Robert Whyte, the two officials in charge of the station, with that open-handed hospitality which the jaded traveller can best appreciate.

So ended my forced march to Nyasa, in which a hundred and twenty miles were covered in a little over four days. This, according to Messrs. Whyte and Taylor, might be considered a "record"; as most white men take at least six days and a half to travel to Karonga's from Fife in a hammock. Altogether, the performance stamps the Zanzibari as a marvel of stamina, more especially when the conditions are taken into account. For three mortal months had these men been trudging from Bunkeya, through swamps and *pori*. At the outset they had barely recovered from starvation and though they passed through a land of plenty before reaching Mweru, half-rations had been the order the day between that and Tanganyika; nor did food abound at Fwambo and the surrounding villages. Yet they accomplished this last spurt, over difficult ground, and with loads, which, thou light in comparison, still averaged a British soldier's kit, without abating a jot of their cheerful perseverance. They were, of course, picked men; thus Mandara, made nyampara for the occasion, had served with Mr. Joseph Thomson, had accompanied Mr. Jackson to Uganda, and had barely escaped the massacre in which Bishop Hannington perished. Also, Akida had been on the Jackson expedition, while Bega went with Mr. Stanley to the relief of Emin Pasha, together with Mirabo Ngumba, whose pluck was displayed so marked during the attack on Msiri's. Still, hardly a pagazi in the caravan would have declined to accompany me, unless absolutely sick; and they be relied upon, besides, to walk until one leg absolutely declined to precede the other.

The *Domira* anchored that night, with Captain Jennings in command, and he promptly supplied the necessary information as to fares and freight. Pending the advent of Captain Stairs, the time passed pleasantly enough; as Raronga's is a busy spot, and, but for its dangerous harbour, might well develop into an important emporium. It has been founded some twelve years, and was the centre of the Nkonde War against the Arabs. Since that time the defences have been strengthened by a Nordenfeldt and a 7-pounder mountain-gun, so that the enslavers would think twice about attacking the position. Within the lines, Mr. Whyte and Mr. Taylor were occupied, on my arrival, in building a very neat European house. The sun-dried bricks, window-frames, and doors, had been constructed by the Wa-Nkonde, under their supervision, and did great credit to the black artisans. Indeed, that intelligent tribe, now reduced to a mere remnant by the slave-raiders, yields to none in the excellence of its handicrafts. Their spear-heads are patterned with many elaborate devices, and their huts ornamented with carvings of considerable finish. Fortunately, British intervention has saved this interesting nation from absolute destruction, though, in other respects, the situation hardly seemed cheerful. The company's officials told me that, with one exception— a Muscat, named Mirambo—the neighbouring Arabs were animated by a most hostile spirit. Also, they were Swahilis to a man, and Swahili spells "slave-dealer." Altogether, I gathered that the traffic had been scotched rather than killed on the northern shores of Nyasa, in May, 1892, though matters were, of course, improving every day.

The Wangoni were another source of disquietude, at that time, which tribe occurs, in scattered settlements, throughout German and British territory. I have already mentioned the bodyguard of those warriors which attended Herr von Siegl at Tabora, and their relatives, living about Karonga's, seemed equally valiant in battle. Their villages lie, for the most part, to the south of Karonga's, and round the township of the powerful chief, Mombera, who has inflicted more than one defeat on the Arabs. Indeed, he was then bent upon retaliation; and, the day after my arrival, runners came into the station with the news that a Wangoni detachment, one thousand strong, was about to attack Malosi's. As the village lay not far from Captain Stairs' march, I sent him warning; though, as a matter of fact, these blacks seldom molest a white caravan. It was annoying to miss the Wangoni on the war-path, since they are said to present a very brave array, with anklets jingling and pipes playing. Some of them, however, came into Karonga's to trade, and still carried their spears and bucklers. The latter were of the oval pattern, which the illustrated papers made so familiar during the war in Zululand; indeed, the Southern Wangoni are believed to have migrated from that country during Chaka's rebellion, nearly eighty years ago. Their missiles seemed comparatively simple compared with those of the Wa-Nkonde, who bear some fourteen different spears of various lengths and weights, including a short two-bladed weapon for stabbing the fallen victim. The latter tribe's military outfit, in fact, bears a curious resemblance to that of an enthusiast at golf.

At 11.30 a.m., on the 14th of May, the caravan arrived, with Captain Stairs looking remarkably well and cheerful. The camp was pitched outside the station, and we proceeded to dispose of our remaining stores and trading-goods to Mr. Whyte. The *Blue Nose* was rather a drug in the market, as Captain Jennings pronounced her to be too light for Nyasa, which lake is subject to violent squalls; but eventually the Administration came to terms. During the day's stay at Karonga's, the men behaved in exemplary fashion, and no case of stealing was reported. On the evening of the 15th, commenced the difficult business of stowing some two hundred obstreperous porters into the *Domira*'s very limited hold, as she lay tossing on a nasty sea. They could not, of course, be allowed on deck, as the vessel would certainly have upset, and even their movements down below caused her to give most unpleasant lists. Eventually they were packed, like herrings in a barrel; and, next day we started, at 6.30 a.m., bound for Ruarwa. With all due respect for the *Domira*, we felt bound to pronounce her a crank craft. Her draught was remarkably shallow, and her bottom resembled a dish. However, the "Lake of Storms", as Livingstone christened Nyasa, belied her name on this occasion; and the wind, instead of rushing through the mountain-funnel, hung far above our heads, round the topmost peaks.

Arrived that evening at Ruarwa, we disembarked the men to eat their dinners and sleep on the shore. The anchorage was indifferent, and the native canoes extremely primitive. Indeed one capsized, and in went the porter Mandara. The sling of his rifle, which was fastened at his back, promptly became entangled about his neck, and kept him under water. As he would most certainly have been drowned, I jumped off the bridge "all standing " and swam to his assistance. Another canoe came up and took him on board, more dead than alive, leaving me to strike out for the *Domira*. There had naturally been little time for reflection, and my return journey had well begun, before I suddenly bethought me that the spot swarmed with crocodiles. The constant apprehension of being seized by the leg and dragged below was most unpleasant, and very glad I felt to grasp the companion and to be hauled up on deck by Hamadi. As for Mandara his gratitude was almost overwhelming, and for the brief remainder of the journey he followed me like a second shadow.

We halted at Bandawé for two days (May 17th to the 19th) to take on board Mr. McCalmont of the Scotch Livingstonian Mission, who was going home on leave of absence with his wife and baby. The last, by his exuberance of health, seemed to have solved the problem if the white race can colonize Central Africa, and I may be allowed to say that the proud father realized one's ideal of the fearless and conscientious evangelist. We visited the mission station, and were much struck by its orderly and thriving appearance. A passenger of a very different sort came on board at Kota-Kota, our next halting-place, in the shape of the notorious Swahili slave-dealer Jumbi. He was accompanied by twelve of his many wives, one of whom, with allowance made for her brown skin, looked remarkably handsome.

Jumbi was a tall, gaunt Swahili, quite seventy years of age, and bore the very worst of reputations. Despite a subsidy of £100 or more from the Central African Administration, he still carried on a large traffic in human merchandise. Indeed, on a recent voyage, the crew of the *Domira* had descried one of his dhows making for the opposite shore, her deck crowded with slaves, and the Union Jack (!) at the masthead. This piece of insolence was in thorough keeping with his daring and unscrupulous character, and he can hardly fail to be a thorn in the Commissioner's side. Jumbi was then about to visit Mr. Johnston, and behaved, accordingly, as if the white man were dearer than his own flesh and blood. Nor did we disturb his composure by disclosing the incident of his crony Yarafua Brahim's intercepted letter. Accordingly he parted with us on the best of terms, though it is quite possible that he emerged from the Johnston interview with a less benign expression upon his shrivelled countenance. For instance, we had evidence that one of the wives, who disappeared after a halt—having gone, said Jumbi, on a visit to her father—had really been sold to another Sultan.

No unusual incident marked the night spent in Monkey Bay; and on the following afternoon we anchored at Mponda's, facing which village stands Fort Johnston. We were most kindly received by Commander Keane and Br. Watson, of whom the latter still suffered from a wound received in the recent Sarifi affair. That unfortunate reverse, it appeared, was due to the cowardice of the native contingent, which fled directly the enemy came in sight. Otherwise the force sent under Mr. King and Dr. Watson, to chastise that petty but marauding chief, would have been fully equal to the emergency. As it was, the Englishmen, with a handful of faithful Sikhs, had to retreat before overwhelming numbers, and were both disabled in the process. Indeed, but for the resourcefulness of the petty officer, who spiked the mountain-gun and led the party home by devious tracks, British prestige might have received a somewhat ugly check. Thanks, however, to the energy of Mr. Johnston, the gun was promptly recovered, and the business simply taught the Administration not to put too much confidence in the nigger ally.

Our voyage down the three hundred and fifty miles of lake concluded, we steamed next morning up its effluent the Shire. Shortly after the *Domira* got up steam, we perceived a boat putting out to meet us, in which sat Mr. H. H. Johnston and Lieutenant

Johnstone, who succeeded Captain Maguire in the command of the Sikh contingent. They had a long talk with Captain Stairs, and congratulated him heartily upon the success of our expedition after which they shook hands, and the steamer forged ahead. For two days we enjoyed the spacious scenery of the Shire, with its broad valley on either bank, bounded by the distant mountains. Without a single hitch we reached Matopé on the 26th, and disembarked for the land march necessitated by the Murchison Rapids.

Here again everything went according to our most sanguine expectations. The men stepped out steadily for the Lunzo, which river runs about halfway between Matopé and Blantyre. As we halted, the McCalmonts, who were being carried, caught up the rearguard, and we lent them an escort of askaris while passing through the caravan. The camp was pitched at 2.30 p.m., and Captain Stairs, who seemed in exceptional vigour, took particular pains to give it an orderly and disciplined appearance. Next day we reached Blantyre at 10.30 a.m., and were met by Captain Sclater of the British Administration, whom we had seen off from Zanzibar nearly a year previously, Mr. Alfred Sharpe the vice-consul, the missionaries, and the traders. After a brief halt, we tramped along an excellent road bordered by trees, past the mission houses, the schools, the flourishing gardens, and the little Gothic Church. Our arrival created a great sensation, as so large a *safari* had never passed through Blantyre before, and the wayside was lined by hundreds of happy and grinning converts. The station has been described so frequently, that I need hardly trouble the reader with my hasty impressions; enough that the first white settlement in Central Africa has been beaten by none of its predecessors in ideal beauty of surroundings or efficiency of practical results.

Two miles and a half only separated us from Mandala, the head-quarters of the African Lakes Administration. Mr. Monteith Fotheringham, the officer present, gave us a camp, and took over a quantity of our superfluous stores. Here we were rejoined by Mr. and Mrs. McCalmont, and, curiously enough, I discovered in Mr. Preston a contemporary at St. Thomas's Hospital. It was a long day's march to Katunga's, where the traveller regains the Shire below its seventy miles of rapids. At this station, named by the way after one of Livingstone's old chiefs, our troubles began. The S.S. *Lady Nyasa* was unable to start, as a rivet in the manhole of her boiler had become loose. Pending the execution of repairs at Blantyre, we had to while away the time by strolling round the plantations and trying, but in vain, to get a shot. Captain Stairs was sorely vexed by the delay, as he longed desperately to get to the coast. Not that he wished to return to a life of ease and quiet in England, though his constitution stood in imperative need of one or two years at least of comparative inactivity. On the contrary, he would have volunteered at once to go to the assistance either of Captain Jacques at Albertville or of Captain Lugard in Uganda. All the suffering and sickness at Fort Bunkeya he had completely forgotten, and his ardent spirit made light of fresh hardships, provided they were accompanied by fresh discoveries and achievements. Upon him the Dark Continent had laid her spell with an absolutely imperious influence.

The mending of the boiler by no means ended our difficulties, for the Lady Nyasa could not carry half our men, and other conveyances had to be procured. Three or four lighters were forthcoming, but even so a company remained unaccommodated, until a large barge was pressed into service. But first it had to be rid of a barrel of tar, and the operation of rolling the heavy mass up a steep bank took over two hours. Such yelling and shouting of orders were seldom heard on the banks of the Shire, and all the while the sun beat remorselessly on our heads. At last, at 5 p.m., the Lady Nyasa was under way, with one of the lighters in tow. It came on to rain, and the stream ran very fast. Before we had gone many yards we could see that the little tub would not answer her helm with so heavy a weight astern. We struck a sandbank; got off; but only to become wedged in the bank more hopelessly than before. The Lady Nyasa could not reverse her engines, and in a trice the lighter came crashing into the side. Needless to say that the Zanzibaris bawled like ten thousand, and it is only right to remark also that their officers felt seriously bedevilled. Eventually, after a scene of the wildest confusion, we took some of the Zanzibaris on board, and turned the rest adrift in the lighter, to paddle down as best they could. Meanwhile the rain descended in torrents, and Captain Stairs was wet to the skin before he could be persuaded to go below. Next day we got off, after a deal of shoving, and began to hope for better things. However, the overloaded boat hardly made satisfactory progress, even when relieved of her follower, and we proceeded with constant bumps and runnings aground. Our advance was woefully slow, and the blue malarious haze which clothed the banks each morning showed, ominously enough, that we had entered the pestilential coast belt. Captain Stairs, however, was bent upon pressing onwards, nor would he wait until the sun's beams had dissipated the vapours. So we reached the limits of British territory at Chiromo, a place that may well become valuable when connected with the Indian Ocean by railway. Hard by a rude iron cross, half-hidden among the rank vegetation, marks the grave of the lamented Bishop Mackenzie.

Near the confluence of the Zambesi with the Shire we passed two British gunboats coming up the former river from Chinde. At Mshamgama we visited the now ruined and deserted hut in which Mrs. Livingstone died, and stood by her grave under a huge baobab tree, while the sun was setting behind the distant Morumballa mountains. On either side of the now opening and now narrowing stream, depressing stretches of sand alternated with reeking mango swamps, until on the 3rd of June we attained Vicenti, a port whose importance has departed with the silting-up of the Qua-qua mouth of the Zambesi. There we disembarked the men, and proceeded to spend a night on shore.

During the last three or four days Captain Stairs was slightly out of sorts, but the symptoms called for no special precautions. He appeared in excellent spirits, and constantly spoke of Zanzibar as the starting-point of future adventures. But before the night had waned, the band of death was upon him. Thanks to the accursed liquor traffic of the Portuguese, the porters obtained large jorums of gin at the Vicenti store. A free fight naturally ensued, and Captain Stairs sent me to stop the infernal pandemonium. I chastised the ringleaders, the more sober professed penitence and for a while quiet reigned. But fresh topers came reeling into camp, and the turmoil broke out anew. Then Captain Stairs went out, and, with the assistance of the chiefs, administered correction to various culprits. The operation took the best part of an hour, and at nine o'clock he retired to rest.

At half-past twelve I was summoned to his bed-side, and found him suffering from haematuria in its gravest form. Next day he was carried on board, and in the afternoon we reached Chinde, at the river's mouth, where, through the kindness of the Administrator, Mr. Hellier, and Mr. Scott, one of the officials, a room was provided in the latter's house. As he lay dying, the ocean's surf could be heard rolling on the bar, and the S.S. *Rovuma* appeared, ready to take us to Zanzibar in the following week. Mr. Robinson was unceasing in his attentions to the sick man, and on the 6th there appeared some hope of recovery. But restless nights undid the work of quiet mornings and constant restoratives; and he expired on the 9th at six o'clock in the evening, the immediate cause of death being a fainting attack from which he could not rally.

Two gentlemen belonging to the London Missionary Society most kindly assisted me to make the coffin, and the funeral took place next day. Captain Stairs was buried in the concession, about three hundred yards behind the African Lakes Company's house. He was, of course, given military honours, the chiefs carrying the bier, preceded by twelve askari and two drummers. The whole white population followed after, and showed the greatest sympathy while the service was being read by Mr. Scott. A wooden cross was placed at the head of the grave, and then, with heavy hearts, we retraced our steps to Chinde.

The rest of the story may be dismissed very briefly indeed. That very day the arrival of the Rovuma, after touching at Beira, brought home to us the full pathos of Captain Stairs' fate, in that he succumbed when so near his journey's end. Still, regret was unavailing, and nothing remained but to embark the *safari*, which operation took place on the 11th. After an uneventful voyage we reached Zanzibar on the 20th; and then proceeded to pay off the men, the Mombasa contingent being conveyed home in the *Juba*. As an illustration of the Swahili's buoyancy of character, I may mention that a considerable body of porters and several chiefs, unwarned by experience, re-engaged themselves within the next few days for the toilsome and arid march to Uganda. On the 5th of July, the Marquis de Bonchamps, Robinson, and myself started homeward bound in the S.S. *Ava*, of the Messageries Maritimes. After bidding farewell to our French companion in Paris, we two Englishmen reached England, safe and sound, on the 23rd; and so another chapter in the history of African discovery was brought to a close.

Bibliography

Crawford, D., *Thinking Black* (London: Morgan & Scott, Ltd., 1912);

Gordon, D., 'Owners of the Land and Lunda Lords: Colonial Chiefs in the Borderlands of Northern Rhodesia and the Belgian Congo', *International Journal of African Historical Studies*, Vol. 34, No. 2. (2001);

Moloney, J. A., 'The Stairs Expedition to Katangaland', *Geographical Journal*, Vol. 2, No. 3. (Sep., 1893)

Oliver, R., review of 'Victorian Explorer. The African Diaries of Captain William G. Stairs, 1887-1892', by Stairs, W. G., and Konczacki, J. M.; *English Historical Review*, Vol. 112, No. 446. (Apr., 1997);

de Pont-Jest, R., *l'expédition du Katanga, d'après les notes de voyage du marquis Christian de Bonchamps*; *Le Tour du Monde*, Vol. LXIV, (1893)

Rotberg, R. I., 'Plymouth Brethren and the Occupation of Katanga, 1886-1907', *Journal of African History*, Vol. 5, No. 2. (1964);

Royal Museum for Central Africa, Brussels, Belgium, *Inventory of the Stanley Archives*, accessed online March 2007, at [http://www.metafro.be/stanley/other_documents/index_html?p=00&b_start:int=45&g=01]

Wilson, A., 'Long Distance Trade and the Luba Lomami Empire', *Journal of African History*, Vol. 13, No. 4. (1972).

Also available from Jeppestown Press:

Where the Lion Roars: An 1890 African Colonial Cookbook
Mrs A. R. Barnes

A reprint of one of Africa's earliest English-language cookery books, dating from 1890. Mrs Barnes' recipes for translucent, aromatic melon and ginger konfyt; fiery curries; and sweet peach chutney are as delicious now as they were a century ago; while instructions for making a canvas water cooler, and for treating snake-bite or fever, offer a fascinating insight into the domestic lives of southern Africa's Victorian colonists. ISBN: 0-9553936-1-2

For full details of our inventory, or to order direct, view our web site at **www.jeppestown.com**

JEPPESTOWN

The Bulawayo Cookery Book and
Household Guide
Edited by Mrs N. Chataway

This reprint of Zimbabwe's earliest cookery book is packed with recipes for Edwardian African delicacies: garnet-coloured tomato jam; fiery, home-made ginger beer and spicy bobotie. Packed with contemporary advertisements for companies like Puzey and Payne, Philpott and Collins and Haddon and Sly, the book even contains a section on veld cookery, contributed by Colonel Robert 'Boomerang' Gordon, D.S.O., O.B.E., who went on to raise and command the Northern Rhodesia Rifles at the outbreak of the First World War. ISBN: 0-9553936-2-0

For full details of our inventory, or to order direct, view our web site at **www.jeppestown.com**

JEPPESTOWN

The Anglo-African Who's Who 1907
Walter H. Wills (ed.)

A reprint of Walter Wills' quirky colonial reference book, containing the details of nearly 2,000 prominent men and women of Edwardian Africa. This astonishing work includes biographies of settlers, soldiers, explorers, politicians and traditional leaders from every corner of the continent. Invaluable for genealogists, historians, military researchers and medal enthusiasts, it offers details of over 1,200 separate medal awards, together with fascinating biographical sketches of colonial African celebrities—many of whom were known personally to the editor. ISBN: 0-9553936-3-9

For full details of our inventory, or to order direct, view our web site at **www.jeppestown.com**

The Rhodesia Medal Roll
David Saffery (ed)

Containing the names of over 12,000 recipients and revealing 2,300 previously unpublished decorations, this definitive book is the ultimate compendium of Rhodesian military and civilian honours and awards gazetted between 1970 and 1981. Fully indexed by surname, it is perfect for medal collectors and dealers, historians and genealogists—and a brilliant heirloom souvenir for recipients and their families. ISBN: 0-9553936-0-4

For full details of our inventory, or to order direct, view our web site at **www.jeppestown.com**

Matabeleland and the Victoria Falls
C. G. Oates (ed)

This book draws on the original diaries, letters, paintings and sketches of Frank Oates to paint a vivid picture of the Victorian exploration of Central Africa. It documents his encounters with legendary rulers such as King Lobengula of the Ndebele and larger-than-life characters like the ivory hunter Frederick Selous, and records Oates' final, fatal trek through the Zambezi Valley towards Victoria Falls. ISBN: 978-0-9553936-4-8

For full details of our inventory, or to order direct, view our web site at **www.jeppestown.com**

10% discount! ORDER FORM

Use this form to order any of our books by post to addresses in the United Kingdom. For overseas orders please use the web site www.jeppestown.com.

Title	Price	Quantity	Total
Where the Lion Roars: An 1890 African Colonial Cookbook	~~£12.95~~ £11.66		
The Bulawayo Cookery Book and Household Guide	~~£12.95~~ £11.66		
The Anglo-African Who's Who 1907	~~£18.95~~ £17.06		
The Rhodesia Medal Roll	~~£17.95~~ £16.16		
Matabeleland and the Victoria Falls	~~£12.95~~ £11.66		
With Stairs in Katanga	~~£12.95~~ £11.66		
Postage and packing within the UK			add £2.80
Total			

To order, send a cheque or postal order for the total amount (made payable to **Jeppestown Press**) to Jeppestown Press, 10A Scawfell St, London, E2 8NG.

Delivery details:

Name:

Address:

Telephone number (in case of query):

www.ingramcontent.com/pod-product-compliance
Lightning Source LLC
Chambersburg PA
CBHW070551160426
43199CB00014B/2462